Lady of the pancham swara
LATA NANI

In Loving Memory of Lata Misra

Lady of the pancham swara
LATA NANI
In Loving Memory of Lata Misra

Cover Design:
Lalatendu Mohanty
Sukanta Paikray

BLACK EAGLE BOOKS
Dublin, USA

BLACK EAGLE BOOKS

USA address:
7464 Wisdom Lane
Dublin, OH 43016

India address:
E/312, Trident Galaxy, Kalinga Nagar,
Bhubaneswar-751003, Odisha, India

E-mail: info@blackeaglebooks.org
Website: www.blackeaglebooks.org

First International Edition Published by
BLACK EAGLE BOOKS, 2026

LADY OF THE PANCHAM SWARA LATA NANI
IN LOVING MEMORY OF LATA MISRA

Cover Design: **Lalatendu Mohanty** | **Sukanta Paikray**
Interior Design: Ezy's Publication

ISBN- 978-1-64560-853-0 (Paperback)

Printed in United States of America

CONTENTS

A Life Dedicated to Culture and Community

Many believe our destiny is written in the stars before our birth. What is doled out to us is something that we perhaps cannot change between the banks of birth and death, but what we chose to make it is what becomes how we are remembered. This book is a tribute to a woman whose talent, grit, beauty and contribution to community went beyond the mundane moments and insurmountable challenges of her life. Srimati Banalata Misra or Lata nani as she was fondly addressed by the Odia brethren of New Jersey worked tirelessly to keep our Odia traditions relevant in a world that often forgets its roots.

The book offers a rare glimpse into the life of a woman who embodied elegance and authenticity and most importantly was a bridge between past and present generations. Through her life she celebrated two joys – the bonds of friendships and community, and that culture to thrive must be lived, celebrated and passed on for posterity Nani's journey from Odisha took her to the other side of the world, yet never distanced her from the cultural roots that defined her. From her early days in Odisha to living a lifetime in America, she remained deeply connected to the traditions of her native land. Through her passion for music and drama—especially the rich classical forms of Champu and Chand—she nurtured a love and pride for Odia culture among the younger and older generation of Odia's residing in North America.

The book is divided into three sections. Part 1: *An Abiding Legacy* details her life growing up in Odisha, followed by arrival in America in the early seventies. Part 2: *A Life in Pictures* shares candid moments from her life that help the reader see and experience the charm and enigma of nani and her ever supporting spouse Sri Saradindu Misra. Part 3: *Lata nani we knew and loved,* is a bouquet of tributes from her extended family- the beloved community members for whom she was mentor, guide and friend.

Born and raised in Odisha, Lata nani grew up in an ambience steeped in songs and folklore typical of the region's cultural heritage. The traditions of Champu—the effortless blending of poetry and music—and Chand, with its lyrical complexity, were not merely cultural recitals to Lata nani. They were symbolic of Odisha's history and traditions. From an early age, thanks to her father's influence, she developed a deep appreciation for these forms, knowing that they carried within them the rich heritage of generations past.

When life eventually brought her to America after marriage, like many immigrants, she had to adapt to a new society, a starkly different way of life, and new responsibilities. Feeling emotionally lost she turned towards her music and culture to moor and ground her innermost self in a land completely different from the one she had known. In those earlier days while singing in homes or a Church setting that hosted Odia gatherings, she realized that cultural traditions can easily fade when communities become apathetic and generations grow up far from their native land. She also realized that Odia classical songs and music were not given the same recognition as Odissi dance, and that community members could easily forget these songs and dramas living far away from the land of their roots.

For her, this realization became her calling, her life purpose. As one of the founding members of the Odisha Society of the Americas, Lata nani began promoting these traditional forms at local community events and years later at the conventions. She understood that for culture to flourish it must be embraced in everyday life and not merely exist in memories and conversations; thus, she went about creating opportunities for the next generation to participate in. With her characteristic determination, she dedicated herself to sharing the beauty of Odia traditions with young people growing up in America. Through music and dramas, she introduced children and young adults to the richness of Champu and Chand. She encouraged and coerced them to sing, recite, and perform, helping them discover not only the medium itself but also the cultural pride associated with it

Her efforts were not limited to teaching. She actively participated and volunteered in cultural gatherings, dramas, and community programs, helping create opportunities and platforms. For many young participants, their first experience of performing traditional Odia music or drama came through her encouragement. Nani believed that culture survives only when it is shared. She found immense fulfillment in seeing young performers learn ancient songs and nuances of Odissi music. For her each new participant was the continuation of a tradition she loved. With a voice that commanded both authority and admiration, Lata nani was the elegant fusion of tradition and modernity, pragmatism and culture. Fashionable, eloquent, and unwavering in her dedication, she showed that preserving culture remains the onus of all community members.

Those who knew her personally also remember that her words could sometimes be sharp, and she never hesitated to express what she believed to be right. She cared deeply about the people and customs she valued, and this resulted in how she communicated with people around her. Her husband and nani were loving hosts and their home was always open for students, friends and community members, the gatherings abundant with music and laughter that brought cheer and a warming pride being bound to one's traditions. Under her guidance, what might have remained foggy recollections of a faraway land became living traditions to experience and appreciate.

In her later years, however, she faced a difficult battle with a degenerative disease. The condition gradually clamped her physical abilities, presenting challenges that would have discouraged many. Yet even in the face of illness, her spirit remained unbroken. She faced the illness with the same strength that had defined her life's work. She confronted the disease with courage, drawing on the strength of her companionship with her husband and the support of innumerable members who loved the couple.

By the time she passed away, her contribution had begun to bear fruit. The songs she taught, the performances she encouraged, and the traditions she helped preserve have not disappeared with her passing. Instead, they continued to live on in the voices and memories of those she had mentored. The program she nurtured has befittingly been renamed to Lata Misra Champu Chhanda Odissi (CCO). Thus, her legacy lies in the pride young members of the community feel when they sing an Odia composition or enact a traditional drama carrying a strong, social impact. For the Odia diaspora, Lata nani's life is a lesson that culture does not survive and thrive without efforts. It survives and flourishes because members choose to carry it forward, with dedication, selfless service and sacrifice.

My grateful thanks to foremost Shashi bhaina, Lata nani's beloved husband who despite his advanced age was full of patience and affection while filling me in on life with his beloved wife. My deep thanks to all the community members who provided me with snippets from nani's life and lastly, I would like to thank our president Sri Nilasundar Jena and the editorial members who held onto the promise voiced on nani's funeral day that her life story will be written in golden words. Special thanks to Mrs. Yasaswini Mohapatra (Annie apa) and Dhanalaxmi Dash (Suja apa) for their invaluable help in supporting this initiative. In the end, her story of purpose discovered and faithfully pursued inspires us all, especially for people like me who had never met nani. This dedication transformed not only her own life but also the lives of many within the community. Lata nani's voice is now silent, but the music she helped nurture will continue to be heard in the voices she trained and compositions she taught for generations to come.

Warm Regards,
Mrs. Deepti Paikray

SECTION 1:

The Abiding Legacy

Ash and soul

It was a bright summer afternoon in 2021, specifically 11th July. Most did not notice huge ship shaped clouds scudding across blue skies. An ordinary day dawned on a beautiful colonial style bungalow in the quiet neighborhood of Franklin township in New Jersey. A huge throng of people had gathered outside the house blooming with roses and summer blooms, the air bedewed with the sweet fragrance of jasmine flowers. However, people wore masks as the shadow of covid lingered in the air. But something was amiss. No loud talk rent the air. Instead, an air of mourning blanketed the house. The main door opened into a spacious living room crowded with people mostly dressed in white or pastels. The furniture was pushed against the wall, and doors and windows were wide open letting in the summer daylight. One was led to think that all was perfect with the mortal world. But alas so was not the case.

Some guests sat quietly with their thoughts, others served water and sweet ginger tea, and yet others grouped together to speak in hushed whispers. When grief rents the air the most commonplace activities give us something to do – small talk, offering snacks and drinking tea are the ones. We are all uncomfortable around grief, worse we do not know how to comfort the one hit hardest by grief, and so doing the routine things gives us a certain grip when our insides feel numb. On a raised wooden table draped in a white cloth was an enlarged photo of an elegant lady draped in an orange sari, her dark, doe eyes looking somberly at the scene of life unfolding before her. She was Srimati Banalata Misra or Lata nani as she was fondly addressed, by the Odia community of New Jersey and New York. Her husband Sri Saradindu Misra, aged 82 years, sits quietly gazing somewhere vague in the distance, for his companion of 52 years has passed away. In his heart there is surely a conundrum between relief that Lata, his wife, is finally free of her acute physical suffering, but also the anxiety as to how he will manage his twilight years without her comforting and lively presence. For many Lata nani was the north star of the community since its inception, guiding the community with her dedication to preservation of the cultural aspects of Jagannath culture. For most members Lata nani and bhaina were the go-to family when they first arrived on American shores. The couple was known for their endearing hospitality and deep connection towards the Odia community they helped nurture and care for.

For a long while a relentless disease ravaged nani's frail body and then covid worsened her condition. Towards the end she could not eat, and the doctor said a tube would be inserted to feed her. Meanwhile, *bhaina* refused to send her to hospice. Instead, he promised the doctor that their own home would be converted into a hospice. They lived a changed life post her ailment their days filled with doctor appointments and physiotherapy sessions to resist and slow down the ruthless march of her ailment. In her last days the always frail nani was administered injections to alleviate her pain as her body lay crumpled like paper on the bed. All the relationships she had tended upon during their lifetime in New Jersey surrounded the couple like a blessing. Knowing her taste for perfection, on her funeral day too everything was arranged the way she would have liked it, from slender white lilies arranged inside crystal vases to bunches of sweet summer flowers in pale colors of lilac and pink flanking her photo.

Lata nani was always pretty with her flawless moon complexion, deep black eyes (that didn't miss the flit of an expression or the pause in a banal talk) beneath carefully tweezed and darkened eyebrows, a slightly haughty aquiline nose, and a winning smile set in a delicate oval face. The fact that she smiled rarely made it that much more special. The woman in the photo has a distant smile, her short hair a rich curtain of black framing dainty features, at peace finally, released from a debilitating disease. Her favorite sandalwood joss sticks are lit in front of her picture and wisps of her earthly persona, and the pure flame of a lamp guides her spirit from the fetters of the mortal world into the expanse of the spirit realm. Births are special, and funerals are momentous too. Births are joyous for a life has come into this world with a light of its own, and funerals, a somber passage of rite that honor the completion of a lifespan and the purpose with which the soul arrived on earth. Death had knocked on this dwelling leaving the vacuum of a voice once heard, a presence that once was, and the only feel that remained in an everlasting mode was the memory of beloved Lata nani.

The gathering remembered how Lata nani fussed over details, loved, used, and appreciated the small luxuries of life and made sure no one left her dwelling without food in the stomach and hope in the heart. Even while on her death bed as life ebbed away from her consciousness, she had a small pedicure done to her feet. And many felt that her fair, beauteous feet indeed resembled those of goddess Mahalaxmi the divine consort of Lord Vishnu. Indeed, she was the goddess of her household, bringing prosperity and joy.

In the fall of 2025, I visited bhaina in the couple's Franklin home for gathering details about his popular spouse. The leaves transitioned into shades of rust and orange, accompanied by a distinct, brisk chill in the air. Franklin in New Jersey is a quiet, laid-back neighborhood with gracious bungalows. Few people were out on their evening stroll as evening gathered in soft, grey hues. Doma, bhaina's caretaker opens the door for me. She welcomes me with a pleasant smile and ushers me in. It is a spacious home mostly done up in white, and huge photos of the couple in happier times and younger years adorn the walls. The furniture is neatly arranged, and a large bed occupies the living room. The house is a bit too quiet, the way homes that hold more memories than members are. I linger in front of the couple's photo and wonder if a little bit of Lata nani's essence lingers on within the frame of their picture together. Bhaina is dashing with his big soulful eyes, a mop of wavy hair and a trimmed down flamboyant moustache that gives him a swashbuckling look. Nani looks petite and demure beside him with an unmistakable air of mystique about her. They look happy within the confines of the photo frame as they were undoubtedly in the expanse of their lives.

Bhaina greets me warmly. Age has been kind to him. He has lost most of his hair but loves to chat with people and has a rosy countenance that belies his 86 years of life. He is seated and welcomes me warmly, is the perfect host and requests me to have some tea and snacks. He too is dealing with age related issues, but talking about his beloved wife warms his voice and his eyes soften as he recounts.

"She was a people's person," he narrates. "Every weekend either we had people over at our home and she would fuss over me and them with her cooking, or we would be at other people's homes. She was at her happiest, chatting with people and cooking for them. Wherever Lata went there would be singing, talk, laughter and food," bhaina recollected mistily, then adds, "now there is only silence." I remain quiet as sometimes the only answer to deep-end questions is silence. Obviously, Lata nani, had figured early on in life that the warp and weft of human relations was essential to the weave of life's fabric.

However, to many members nani was a paradox of traits that ranged from sudden abrupt mood swings that resulted in a sharp retort to gushing, hospitality that warmed the cockles of the guest's heart. Also, she never liked being called Banalata or mausi. She liked being called Lata or maximum Lata nani. Most agree that with nani if she offered you a hand then that's all you took, you really couldn't grab the arm. That was nani. She did keep people on toes around her. She was also very practical, resourceful and a wonderful manager of things. Thus, bhaina was fine with her handling the everyday business of life and he just watched her with a quiet affection.

"We had our moments and argued mercilessly like any other married couple. You couldn't win with her," he adds with a twinkle in his eyes. "But we could not remain angry with each other for long. Besides, somebody or the other was always dropping home. And then we could not sulk in front of them, could we?" he gurgles with a soft laugh.

Her delicious and authentic food from fish to chicken curries was the talk of the community. Lata Nani made the best *rasgullas* but wouldn't share her recipe with anyone. Amazingly, they were all the same size dunked in a bath of sugar water. When you bit into one it just dissolved into your mouth leaving a spongy flavor of sweetness tinged with rose water. After numerous years of togetherness, she finally shared it with two community members. "But we still cannot make them as spongy soft as she did," comes the candid confession.

Friends always dropped in to check on the couple, and their steadfast presence helped the couple through the days when bhaina knew that his wife was slipping away. During her last days when nani wanted only tea and mango pulp then a dear caring friend fed her only that knowing that she was soon going to pass over the veiled threshold.

Known for her exemplary talent, outstanding contribution to Odisha Society of America for keeping the tradition of champu chand and drama alive, Lata nani would have been happy to see the attention to detail lavished upon her funeral ceremonies. She was bathed, then dressed in a beautiful sari and adorned lovingly as a married woman with the vermillion dot adorning her fair forehead and filled in the parting of her hair, for one last time for her beloved husband.

Suja apa, nani's niece (daughter of nani's eldest sister) who resides in Bhubaneswar, recollects that even during her last stages of failing health and her very last trip to Bhubaneswar in 2019 she was always concerned about her husband, instructing Suja apa to unfailingly offer water to Lord Shiva's linga. It was her strongest wish that she passes away a married woman, and that's what happened.

She remembers her aunt as a very active and dynamic lady oozing confidence in her thinking and action. Many people do not know that nani was born in critical circumstances, with her legs coming out first at childbirth. Later many people in the village came to be healed from her from various pains and aches by getting their body part touched by little Lata's legs.

When I ask Suja apa about her initial impressions of her aunt, she mentions that from day one she was always perfectly turned out, always interested in clothes, make-up and fashion and wanting to travel the world. She would frequently reprimand her niece's simple appearance and ask her to add more colors to her wardrobe and life. She arrived at her niece's house, opened her wardrobe, and flicked through all the saris that she expected to be arranged like colorful compartments of a fashion train.

"Here wear this one" she would say authoritatively, "this would add some color to your face."

"Even when I visited her in her Franklin home in 2015, she made me wear one of her saris to an OSA gathering. She just liked people wearing their best clothes and looking their best and could instinctively figure out the sari, make up and accessories."

She further adds, "My aunt was of very independent mentality and did not let anyone talk her down." Laughingly, she recollects, "She would frequently reprimand my father if he ever ventured to scold my mother."

Thus, for nani outer beauty was the portal to the inner efficiency of matters of life, work, and home. Perhaps it was her way of rebuffing life that threw some deep disappointments at her and then later cramped her body and spirit within the cage of an acute illness. Maybe when she dressed up to make herself happy and charm the world, it did not let the disappointments of life fester inside her and bhaina's shared life. And therein then lies a life lesson learnt from her indefatigable spirit that external appearance of a person is as important as the generosity of soul, for it is a fact of life that people especially women gauge us on our initial appearance. For a famous celebrity once mentioned that beauty is only skin deep and isn't that deep enough.

Everyone knew how fond nani had been of dressing and no effort was spared for her last journey, as garlands and exotic flowers were arranged aesthetically around her picture even as arrangements were made to carry her body to the funeral home. People reminisced how she would turn up elegantly dressed up for every occasion, her hair and make-up perfectly done with a dab of her favorite perfume adding to her eyes on me aura.

Of course, these dear ones had also been wary of her blunt and forthright manner with some having been at the receiving end of a volley of rebukes from nani. As a few recalled when she had first arrived on the American shores, she struck fear in many people's hearts owing to her elemental nature to say things in too direct a fashion. Many times, members would get upset with her but beyond the sharpness of her speech existed a giving and affectionate heart that loved people, gatherings, songs, food and laughter and above all Odia culture. Over the years when she saw how family friends took care of them, she mellowed down and appreciated their steadfast presence as a true blessing of Lord Jagannaath.

Although the couple did not have children of their own, here everyone was a family whose life had been touched by nani and bhaina in some manner that bought sweet memories and recollections on this day. Many of these friends had formed a ring of caretakers who took turns dropping in on the couple, and helped them in their daily life with medication, food, and small talk. Everyday talk, conversational talk is so important. It's just something that draws people closer, enables our spirits to knock on each other's doors and helps us live our lives feeling less alone and isolated in a world obsessed with speed, achievement and urgency. Nani was known for her frequent and weekly calls to all the people she considered family and friends, just to check that all was fine with their world, and if it was not then a dish of fish curry and pitha was promptly dispatched. When there were emergencies, people turned up at their door at any hour of the day. This was the community that members had nurtured and that offered care, compassion and a sense of belonging to all especially bhaina and nani during their most challenging times. It was thus befitting that all members of Odisha society gathered that day in July and instead ordering food to feed the assembled after the rites were over, decided to cook food at Lata Nani's home to feed the grieving multitudes.

Nani never let anyone leave her home without feeding them, thus in her memory the guests fed each other. She truly believed that food renders solace, comfort, and joy. Thus, for Lata nani feeding people was not merely an act of appeasing their hunger but a deeply spiritual need that nourishes the spirit of the host and the guest. The kitchen fires were lit and a simple meal of rice, *dalma* (lentils with vegetables) and *bhaja* (crispy vegetables) was fed to all.

As a member recounted that Nani was a perfectionist and her bhaja was delectable. She was sharp to point out that if you do not first let the utensil warm, then let the oil warm and not burn, then only will the mix of cumin, fennel, fenugreek and mustard seeds crackle and the bhaja be crisp and stir fried.

Over the next few days, the extended Odia family also kept food outside to feed the spirit of the ancestors. Lata nani was gone. No more would her beauteous voice ring like temple bells over her home and the life of her loved ones. No more would she step out in her Fab India kurtas or American tops her hair styled fashionably, and makeup carefully done. No more would she fuss over her guests. No more would she make sure that her singers got the best performing slot at conventions. She was only seventy-two when the great puppeteer ruling the skies pulled her string of life.

One by one people left the Franklin Park home that had housed the couple for almost two decades. Few still hung back to give consolation and comfort to the bereaved spouse. Strangely the plants that nani had nurtured too missed her. A jasmine plant that she was particularly attached to shriveled up the day she passed away. Death is final but life too has a say, especially a life lived with authenticity that had made Nani turn the page of each new day and greet it with a smile and a purpose. Outside it was a clear blue firmament dotted with immense moving clouds. Verily one of the cloud ships must have carried her soul across the ocean of what she had been, to merge into the final, blissful truth epitomized by the lotus feet of Lord of the Universe, Lord Jagannath himself. However paradoxically, Lata nani forever lives within the mellifluous notes rendered by the young talent she nurtured in the tradition of champu chand and the numerous hearts she touched within the Odia community. Moreover, the shared love and life of bhaina and nani is a remarkable life story for the younger generation about commitment, affection and sanctity of married life that embraces the vagaries, setbacks, and joys of human life. ■

Whispers from a Village life

"You are not born a star you become a star. A star is born with that indefinable extra something."

Lata nani was born on June 1, 1949, in a village called Nariso near Cuttack into a conservative, brahmin family. Altogether they were five siblings and nani was the youngest. Her father was Late Sri Nidhi Sarangi and mother Srimati, Durga Sarangi. Her father was an Agriculturist cum Community Activist. In the family she was very close to her mother as well as two elder sisters. She had two elder brothers. Being the youngest child, she was very affectionate to all. An interesting incident marked her birth though causing great pain to her mother. Nani was born legs first and for a long-time people of her village came to her believing that a touch of her leg would heal them of back pain and other painful issues of the body.

Nani's father held a modest job, and mother was of course tied down with dawn to dusk household work. It was a quiet village, and the family had trouble making ends meet, but there were coconut and banana trees all around, fish in the pond, stacks of rice in the kitchen and love to splurge all around, especially on little Lata who was naughty as a skittish calf. Although wealth of a silver and gold hue was sorely lacking, a different kind of richness was abundant in the simple household—of knowledge and resilience in a tenuous, mortal world. India had gained its freedom, and the winds of change swept every nook of the country. All the siblings went to school. However, growing up in a large household with meager means young Lata learned the life lessons of frugality and the treasure of human relationships.

Lata nani's niece, Suja apa is kind enough to talk to me from Vrindavan despite a terrible cold and fever. Suja apa's mom was the eldest, followed by another sister and nani was the youngest. "Our grandfather was a good singer and was involved in many cultural programs in his village. Every evening, he would read an excerpt from the Bhagwat Geeta and sing champu chand." It was a strong belief that following ancestral customs and traditions purifies one's soul. Unknown to her little Lata's life was being prepared in a mysterious way. Her little heart and ears became tuned to the melodies floating about their modest home and soon she garnered attention because of her mellifluous voice. Because of his motivation during early days, she developed interest in music and sang different traditional and classical songs. Also, her interest in Odia language was deep and she was to later on take it as a main subject in college.

From childhood Lata loved to sing simple village songs, and the notes of her young, tinkling voice filled her home's cobbled courtyard with grace coming from the munificent skies. A grace that would take her to distant shores, a grace that would be sufficient to see her life through with a loving partner despite the sharp sting of thwarted dreams that life would also bring, a grace that would make her travel the world and form new bonds and relationships. All through her growing years Lata wanted to travel, a wish that manifested into a reality for an earnest desire and its fulfilment are indeed yoked together by a ever listening universe.

Once she told a dear friend all misty eyed.

"To go to school, I had to wade through a river or drown in it," she said laughingly. Somehow there would always be a river to cross in her later years, and she of course chose to cross it with strength, integrity, and dignity rather than drown in the waters of self-pity and why did it happen to me rumination.

Meanwhile, many silver moons later little Lata had now blossomed into a pretty, young girl. Fair of countenance, her hair was black silk, but what stood out in a dainty face were her large, black eyes that viewed the world with a certain innocence that stemmed from the pool of a simple albeit curious heart. Wedding proposals began to come into her life. One day a family came to see her. One elderly member came and spoke to her at length about her interests in life. Young Lata had just returned after giving her intermediate exams. Without reservation she patiently answered the thespian's queries. Remember it was the seventies decade when women were still timid and reluctant to share their views, but not Lata nani. She also impressed the older man with her soulful singing.

Little did she know that it was her future husband's family that had come to see her. Bhaina tells me with a twinkle in his eye that his family had rejected 6 other girls. He was much sought after, despite the fact that they were not rich, as bhaina's family was well known in Orissa. They were married on May 25th, 1969. Nani was at the time twenty years old and bhaina 30 years old.

"She absolutely floored my father with her confidence," says Saradindu bhaina with a soft chuckle that echoes around a home in New Jersey the walls of which are adorned with photos of his life partner, now gone. " I am not remembering but she also narrated an entire poem of either Sri Radhanath Ray or Radha Mohan Gadanayak. Not for a moment did she hesitate to answer any questions posed to her.

A moment later, he says softly.

"I miss her terribly. With her around me there was never a dull moment. Despite our petty fights and arguments. She cared for me and I depended upon her. Now our house is silent and I myself do not know what I am waiting for."

I mumble small words of comfort at a loss of words myself. Bhaina too is braving health issues plagued by the absence of his beloved wife. But talking about his wife brings a gentle warmth to those eyes that have seen the world.

"Your bag is smart. He tells me. It's a rectangular Michael Kors that fits my wallet, notepad, and pencil. "She would have loved your bag. For she loved matching her saris to her bags and not the other way around. When she died everything was gifted away, her saris, her jewelry, and her bags."

"And who gifted her all this?" I ask.

"Well of course me," he says laughingly and with pride

"and then she bought some on her own. I think she liked to dress up for me," and I smile at the affection in his voice, amazed at a relationship that most can only dream of.

Many others also reinforce that nani pampered mausa through her cooking. No one taught her how to cook but she picked it up naturally. Like all other things in her life, she was a terrific cook and host. However, mausa was her life and she loved to fuss over him.

A fact corroborated by other friends of the couple who tell me that she kept a note of each person's likes and dislikes and always kept a small portion of their favorite food, dishing it out as a special surprise – from fish and chicken curry to mouthwatering desserts like kheri and rasgulla. It was her life philosophy to do all things big or small to the very best, and in this way built more affection amongst the community members through the web of interconnections and codependency.

At the time of their marriage bhaina worked in a modest job for accountant general in Bhubaneswar, after completing his Bachelor of Arts. Meanwhile, Lata nani completed her matriculation from Niali High School and then joined Ramadevi Women's College in Bhubaneswar and completed her Bachelor of Arts in history and political science. Bhaina's family too had meager means and young Saradindu desired to stretch his wings and give a better life to himself and his partner. What made matters difficult for the young couple was that bhaina's mother was a stepmother who did not really make conditions easy for nani. They were desperate to escape their small and constricted existence.

Soon destiny came knocking in the form of an American Jewish family. They had come from Harvard University and bhaina helped them in their research work. One day, with hope thumping strongly in his heart bhaina asked the couple if he and his wife could come to USA.

They replied in the affirmative and promised to manage all the visa application process, the gracious couple replied. They owned a belt company called Ajaks and it was here that bhaina worked on coming to America. It was the early 1970's and the process was not as stringent as now. All documentation was done, and then the inevitable happened.

Bhaina bid adieu to his motherland and arrived on the shores of the great America in 1972. A year later nani joined him. At the very outset the girl from the village loved America. She loved the wide asphalt roads, the fancy cars whizzing by that did not honk and overrun passengers, women in modern clothes with makeup and manicured nails, sprawling homes with tidy gardens and two car garages. Above all, the country offered her a life of independence and freedom, far away from the fetters of staying within the confines of her in-law's family and limited financial resources. Many years later she would tell a friend.

"When I sang in the village home at times, I got this strange feeling that I was meant to be somewhere else. That something far beyond was beckoning me. What it was I didn't know, but now I do." Lata nani loved to travel beyond borders and now fate finally gave her the opportunity to.

■

Spreading wings

Thus, the young couple arrived in the land of liberty and opportunity with excitement buzzing through their veins. But stars in the eyes and a stare with eyes wide open modernity of America could not of course fill bellies nor offer a roof over their head. In the early 1970's the number of Odias in America was very few. There was no formal organization of OSA as exists today with over 450 members all connected through WhatsApp's groups. In those days of no mobile phones' nana and nani desperately reached out to the few Odia families residing in New York. This is where the very pragmatic side of nani's personality would serve like a layer of accepting soil open to opportunities of friendships and jobs, and doing away with the vagaries and weeds of doubt and isolation with a determination to live the American Dream.

At that time Dr. K. M. Das was the father of Odia society. Every weekend 5-6 Odia families gathered at his home over the weekends to bond over rice, fish curry, mashed *choka* (mashed potatoes with onion and chillies) and talk about life in America and their homeland, the latter now existing only in their memories. At the invitation of Dr. Das, bhaina and nani lived in his house for a year in Cambria Heights, New York. Dr. K. M. Das had come to America in 1958, completed his master's and PhD in pathology, and became chief of staff at New York's Animal Medical Center, besides joining the Regional Supervisor of veterinarians on the East Coast. His son, Dr. Annada Das, who has long been a physician in New York, recollects those days.

"Along with Shashi bhaina, I went to pick up Lata Nani at the Kennedy airport. I was in 9th grade at that time and remember she fitted so well with our family. Bhaina spoke to me like a friend. The first, informal Odia Society was formed in our home in Cabria Heights. A group of Odia families who lived and worked in New York met at our home every weekend."

He further recollects that his father frequently requested Lata nani to sing and she obliged gladly.

"She was not shy and never hesitated. In fact, she later frequently sang devotional songs at The Hindu temple in Flushing, New York which is the oldest temple in America. They also had friends in Columbia University and hosted a radio program. They were not used to this nuclear family trend in America, and thus actively reached out to make friends and stay connected with the Odias in the vicinity."

The families remained closed and many years later when bhaina and Lata nani bought a home in Little Neck, the Das family was again close neighbors residing in Manhasset.

"Nani was so lively and she attended all OSA gatherings. She was never shy and loved to perform. In her later years when suffering from the disease she was on walker, then on a wheelchair. However, Nani was not the person to get fazed with life's challenges, and till the time she could she attended all the OSA conventions and gatherings. Still, she suffered a lot. They always trusted me with all medical advice, and I am just so glad that we could live together in joy and trust for such a long time."

As chance would have it, I came across an article published on Lata nani in Orissa Post in April 2019. In a telephonic chat, she talked about her passion for Odissi music and what drove her to work towards popularizing it. In Lata Nani's words: "I learnt the nuances of Champu, Chhanda and Odissi vocal by following my father and brother when they practiced these forms. I could sing Odissi music with clarity when I was barely five. Be it Republic Day or Independence Day, my teachers always asked me to recite the national anthem in my school. A school inspector named Raghunath Patnaik used to call me during his visit to the school every time and ask me to sing. When I was in Class IX, I played the character of Jayadev, the poet who composed Gita Govinda. Not only did I play the character, I rendered my voice for the tracks of the play titled Jayadev. I could never think of a life without music."

She further expressed," Stalwarts like Balakrushna Das, Shyamamani Patnaik and Bhikari Bal devoted their entire life for the growth of Odissi music. But after them, these forms seemed to be disappearing and there was an urgent need for revival."

After arriving in America and needing money to sustain themselves both nani and bhaina began to work in the belt factory of the American Jewish people responsible for bringing them to America. After some time bhaina left this work and joined a publishing house even as nani continued to do odd jobs to bolster the finances of the young couple.

Bhaina recollects, "At the very outset Lata loved America, the way women were given equal economic rights appealed to her forthright nature. The fact that there were so many options to dress and do makeup. She loved cosmetics- lipsticks, nail color, creams, and perfumes. And as we slowly began to get to know each other, I realized she is a people's person and is the happiest surrounded by a bevy of buzzing Odia's. "Thus, at heart she remained an Odia very attached to her homeland's cultural roots."

In the years to come, Lata nani became very independent and managed all things big and small, which bhaina was only too happy to relegate it to her. At small informal gatherings she loved to talk about drama and singing, and the talk itself nourished everyone's soul. A year later, seeking more privacy and desiring to be on their own, they moved from the residence of Sri K M Das to a one-bedroom apartment near Central Park in New York. This too was rented out to them by the American Jewish family they had worked for.

"It was a brown heavy stone building, and we paid the princely rent of $125 per month. This was in the mid 70's. Despite the posh locality Lata did not fancy it as we had to climb to the third floor to our apartment and secondly, she felt lonely as there were no Odias in the area. However, we were happy in each other's company and Lata was the perfect companion, humorous and friendly.

We were young and romance for us always hung out in the most mundane of activities. Besides, we were living in one of the finest cities of the world, earning our own money and that was a heady feeling to sink in."

Then in the late 1970's they moved to Brooklyn, the other very far end of New York on the insistence of Odia's friends who resided in the area.

"It was again a small apartment with big mouses," bhaina chuckles as he relates. "We did not have a phone but the happiness when friends dropped over was immeasurable. Everyone was working so it was always potluck. Unknown to them, this first lot of ambitious, determined, and hardworking Odias were actually laying down the basis of a community that would expand and widen into a formal community of Odias on the east coast in the forthcoming years.

Famous American cook Laurie Colwin strongly believed that food filed stomachs and hurting hearts. In her words, "The table is a meeting place, a gathering ground, the source of sustenance and nourishment, festivity, safety, and satisfaction. A person cooking is a person giving: even the simplest food is a gift."

Shashi bhaina recollects that his wife could cook anything, but she was most sought after for her fish, chicken gravies and desserts. Also, whatever she cooked never fell short.

"People were just drawn to Lata the way moths are drawn to light, her mannerisms, her sense of fashion, the way she piled them with food. She created a small home wherever we went."

Meanwhile, yet again they had to move into a slightly bigger apartment in Queens when bhaina was joined by his brother-in-law, sister and their daughter. Family relations were always important to them and in whatever way they could they supported their loved ones "My brother-in-law got scholarship to study in Hawaii, but he was allowed to complete it locally. We took the decision to stay together and moved to a bigger apartment in Queens, where we lived for 2 years. It was a happy time for us bonding with family from India."

After they left the couple finally bought their first house in Queens in Little Neck.

"For 13 years we made that small but beautiful house our home. It was strategically located near highways and the train station so I could easily travel to Manhattan and Lata to the sundry jobs she undertook. Working and contributing to the home finances was very important to her. Besides, we never forgot our meagre growing up years and were eager to earn and savor the freedom that America offered."

Bhaina recollects "We were amongst the first Odia's in the NY NJ area in the early seventies." At that time there was no OSA group. We just casually met in people's homes and celebrated Saraswati pooja at a church or a temple. Lata always made sure with others that there was plentiful food available and then later she began to sing on these occasions. One day she was touched when a girl sang champu chand on stage. That moment connected her to where she came from and her father's musical influence on her.

A wire of memory twanged within Nani's heart. In that instant her life gained a vital purpose. She began to sing champu chand and participate in dramas. Going forward at events like Saraswati pooja she began to involve the younger generation, generously and patiently teaching them the finer nuances of Odia song compositions. Somehow, she felt responsible for keeping people connected to their cultural roots. It also filled her life with a measure of joy as the couple could not have children of their own. Also, she observed that Odias living in the US never took Odissi music seriously in comparison to Odissi dance. She persuaded OSA to include Champu and Chhanda in its annual function, a few took interest in it. She left no stone unturned to make Odias realize that Odissi sangeet is no less captivating than Odissi dance. In the year 2009, ten Odia youngsters, ranging from eight to 18 years, were persuaded to learn Champu, Chhanda and Odissi to perform in the 2009 OSA convention. They sang brilliantly to the joy of the audience and soon champu chand and Odisi music became an integral part of OSA conventions and functions. As a befitting tribute to nani's relentless efforts the program in 2019 officially became the *Lata Misra Champu Chhanda Odissi (CCO).*

On another note, the thing with Lata nani was that if she met you once she wouldn't just let you slide by. You had entered her cosmos, and she would keep you in her orbit by calling up on weekends, keeping everyone's likes and dislikes of food and other sundry things in her mind, making sure that someone in your family was participating in the cultural activities. Initially many were wary of her because of her strong rebuffs but later warmed to her inherent warmth and giving personality.

Bhaina tells me, "At that time there was no rath yatra celebration or Kumar Poornima, nor the annual picnic which is now celebrated. We just met in someone's house or a church or temple, ate, chatted, and sang. At the back of our minds was always the question that how we do Odias strengthen our presence and connection on foreign shores. Then the first annual meeting was held in 1973, and the group began to register new members and slowly the umbrella of OSA began to include all newcomers".

The entire Odia community is grateful for Nani's biggest contribution towards the propagation and preservation of champu chand in the classical Odia music genre. In 2009 when the convention was held at Trenton in New Jersey, Lata nani coerced the legendary singer Sri Sikandar Alam's daughter Nazia Alam to record Champu Chanda on CDs. She then convinced people to buy these CDs, in order to support their traditions, and further instructed Mrs. Riti Mohanty (a wonderful singer herself) to begin to teach champu chanda to the younger generation of Odia society. Champu chanda competitions were arranged by her and thanks to her tireless efforts Champu Chanda was integrated into all OSA conventions and continues to delight the audience up to the present day.

Bhaina says with fondness, "she would keep a keen eye out on the performers list and frequently call up people to convince their children to perform and adopt the traditional singing art of Odisha. She felt and rightly so that if the tradition was not passed on it would die a sure death." Lata nani could not take it that a tradition so ancient should die on the altar of modernity, ignorance, and materialism. For her, a life without music was incomprehensible.

Undoubtedly, Lata nani was a multi-faceted personality excelling in all spheres of her life with her keen and curious mind. She had seen frugality while growing up in the village in Bhubaneswar. She understood the importance of money and took up jobs to support their life in America. From the start she had no issues in adapting to the American work culture and accepted various jobs like accounting, sales etc. reveling in the financial independence and worldly exposure these professional outings bought her. In fact, she was proud of her feminist outlook that was an unbeatable combination of stunning appearance and sharp pragmatism. This facet of her personality was explicitly revealed in her surprisingly spontaneous performance in Sri Fakir Mohan Senapati's drama, "Patent Medicine." Nani convincingly portrayed the role of Sulochana, a woman who is aware of her husband's philandering ways and decides to teach him a harsh lesson by beating him with a broom. Many felt that nani could essay the role so wonderfully owing to her naturally fiery spirit that would at no cost tolerate any wrongdoing.

Life is always a criss cross of setbacks, obstacles, and moments of joy. The former tends to be bigger, and the latter are mere sparks that render us with the happy strength to go through what destiny has ordained for us. Most of the time, strength and wisdom lie in not fighting what fate has quartered us with but accepting our lot with fortitude and not resignation. Bhaina and nani were denied the pleasure of having their own children but they bore this with stoic resolution as the supreme will of Lord Jagannaath. They had each other, and a beautiful home replete with plants, food, and friends where the evenings were lit up with the lamp of faith before the little Krishna in her altar, and the walls resounded with sounds of music and gaiety.

Nani strongly felt that being Odia did not mean being restricted to Odisha but in its most authentic way an Odia could be miles away from their homeland, contribute towards their own family and America's progress and yet always remain true in spirit to their beloved Odisha by following the native land's traditions. Also, at a different level she was able to look deep within herself, so deep that she had to look past the layers of obstacles and self-pity and discover her purpose and in finding that purpose she was able to heal herself of deeper disappointments and keep moving forward.

"She kept our home beautifully and managed it most efficiently. We would rise early, drink tea and after a light breakfast leave for our work. Evenings were about talking, arguing, eating dinner and planning meet ups with our friends. I never won an argument with her," bhaina laughs softly. "However, she had no patience for the egoistic lot and never entertained them in any fashion. I guess diplomacy was never inside her but she more than made up for it by creating a home anywhere and everywhere we went."

In the 1980's they bought their second home on Dix Hills, Long Island after selling the home in Little Neck. Bhaina had completed his Master of Science from Brooklyn Polytechnic, and both lived a prosperous life for 21 years in this home. This was a bigger home than the one in Queens. Bhaina went on to become a successful accountant. Then again before retirement they moved to South Brunswick as there were more Odia people in New Jersey and finally moved into their current home in Franklin in 2005 where they lived a long and fruitful life until her passing away in 2021. They were looking forward to spending their retirement life in peace when dark shadows gathered on the horizon of their twilight years.

■

In the light and shadows of life

Life can be likened to a vast field where everyone must tread their own path. There can be no one way of travelling but of course one must only move forward. Did bhaina and nani feel fulfilled and successful? Well, success for them was what they had intensely hoped for and dreamt of which is travelling beyond the confines of their situations and home country did come true. They were able to carve out a fulfilling and prosperous life for themselves in America, but fulfillment also came from the acceptance of fate's vicissitudes which none of us can sidestep and detour from. Bhaina and Lata nani could never become parents and there might have been a place in her heart that naturally craved to become a mother.

"Yes, the disappointment was always there. She worried who we would lean upon and who would look after us in our old age. But she learned to channelize that weight of unfulfilled, nurturing energy towards other outlets, like teaching children champu chand and slowly with her gregarious and extroverted nature the Odia community became our extended family. She was a friend to all and had an opinion to give on all matters. And always her practical and outgoing nature became the bedrock of our life. We travelled to beautiful locales around the world and met up with our dear ones in India." So, the phone rang in their home, the front bell chimed frequently, the kitchen fires were regularly on as dal ma and fish curries simmered, and laughter rebounded from the walls. If anyone was sick food was sent from their kitchen, if anyone did not show up at gatherings a check-in phone was made to find out about the person's whereabouts. Nani and bhaina were celebrating an ordinary life for as long as they could which remains certainly a measure of authentic success.

A community member recollects that even during her last days nani did not fail to find out why her offspring was not performing on stage. For nani believed everyone could sing and perform. Perhaps nani had been able to figure out that life was a somewhat generous imbalanced equation of sharing our talents, nurturing young minds, accepting the vagaries of fate, and most importantly living in the present be it in New Jersey or visiting her sisters and nieces in India. There would be very dark spaces in her life, especially an oncoming degenerative disease, but as long as she could she held onto the goodness that every ordinary day offered in the company of her beloved husband and being able to live at fully functional level of physical health and mental sharpness. I ask bhaina if nani was spiritual.

"She was religious and would often adorn baby Krishna with new clothes, offer a lamp and offer brief prayers at dusk time. However, she believed more in performing actions in life and moreover when she sang it was an offering of complete love and adoration. She genuinely believed that our natural talents help further our homeland's traditions, and that performing instils in us a strong cultural pride."

Nani loved the pleasures of life, and this included travel. Once they had gone to Hawaii for a wedding. On the return journey she found that she could not walk at all. On returning to New Jersey, they frantically contacted numerous doctors and even specialists in India but to no avail. Nani was diagnosed with Parkinson. Parkinson's disease (PD) is a chronic, progressive neurological disorder affecting movement, causing tremors, stiffness, slow movement (bradykinesia), and balance issues, with symptoms worsening over and unfortunately has no cure. Slowly the disease severely restricted her movements and two years later she had to quit her job.

Bhaina recollects that "Even when she went for therapy, she was immaculately dressed; her toenails pained a beautiful blushing pink and a whiff of flower perfume announcing her presence. She really knew no other way to live this one life."

She tried to fight the disease and tried to continue doing the daily household chores herself but at last had to surrender to the ravages of the disease. At this time the couple's circle of friends from the Odia community rallied around them. Around this time, they also hired a house help Doma who became an invaluable resource to them.

With therapy nani felt better. When her niece Suja apa and her husband visited them in 2015 Lata nani was wheelchair bound but still she had no caretaker, she cooked food for all when they visited them in New Jersey and together, they saw the beautiful gardens in Pennsylvania. She loved flowers and often dreamt of taking flower seeds back from India to USA. Travelling was her other hobby and again in 2017- 2018 she travelled to Goa and Hyderabad with bhaina.

When I query apa how the relation between her aunt and her better half was she smilingly reminisces,

"She always loved to travel, and he pampered her so much. They loved gifting and receiving tokens of affection. I remember when my aunt was married, I was a little child, and they gifted me a sweet pink ruffled frock. She bought us cosmetics and bedsheets from America, and once also bought a beautiful chikan sari for me.Two years after their marriage mausa gifted nani a beautiful organza sari in the hue of a sun orange color. Once while going out my aunt was attempting to drape the sari and mausa held the pleats patiently, and once she had draped it to perfection his eyes said it all. They made such a handsome couple."

Meanwhile even after the ailment, the couple continued to visit their loved ones in India every two years. And as a strange twist of fate also purchased a flat in Chandrasekharpur that was furnished as per their choice. A caretaker took care of this apartment but as destiny had ordained the couple could only live in this home for a couple of times.

"Little did she know that 2019 was the last time she would visit Bhubaneswar," recollects Suja apa sadly. Even though severely affected by Parkinson she was still so concerned about mausa. Although she also desired to pass away as a married woman."

"Promise me you will offer water to Lord Shiva's linga for the wellbeing of mausa," she would request with a quiet desperation. Perhaps her soul whispered to her an unknown language in the darkness of night that her days on this earth were soon going to end. Then one day there was a terrible accident in Bhubaneswar. She fell in the bathroom and a torrent of blood gushed from her forehead. Nani was taken to KIM's hospital where the stitches took two to three hours. In that moment she knew that she could no longer live in the present. In that moment she had to surrender to the powerful forces tugging at the dance of life and death.

Nani said to her niece, "Suja this is my last visit to Bhubaneswar. I cannot come again." They kept in touch over the phone but there came a day when they could no longer talk as the disease took away her speech too. The song of Lata nani's life dimmed and fluttered inside the cage of her body. Loved ones dropped in to chat, recite religious texts or just sat with bhaina in silence. Her soul struggled to break free from its painful captivity. The husband and wife spoke with the pain and love in their eyes. Bhaina no longer being able to see the suffering of his beloved wife conveyed to her that it was time for her to go.

Her beloved niece Suja apa called her one day, her niece with whom she had innumerable memories of traveling, dressing, and sharing secrets. But all nani could do was hear her niece's voice. It would be the last time they interacted. Nani passed away on 11th July 2021, a day before Gundicha yatra.

Our incredibly gifted Lata nani perhaps led a most ordinary life but then she always did that little extra that imbued the ordinary with a little extra- cooked someone's favorite dessert, changed her nail color every 6 days, called up to find why a young person was not participating in performances or just called people to know if they were doing well on the road of life. She did that little extra that made her ordinary days vibrant with an extraordinary sheen of life well lived. In her words," "My husband also loves Odia music and drama. He stood by me and encouraged me at every step. Getting the love and care of several Odia families and being engaged with several cultural activities, we feel there is so much more we can do."

Perhaps the biggest lesson we can learn from nani and bhaina's life is to keep moving forward no matter what challenges life may bring. That the most precious wealth is those of friends and of living life in the present and making things happen instead of waiting for them to happen. That the community we have nurtured will always stand by us. Just maybe nani's soul agreed to some tough life lessons before descending on this earth and when it exited her mortal coil someone up there must have clapped hard for her resilience for showing up on days that worked and days that did not. Most importantly Lata nani and bhaina will always be remembered for building a community that is not only a group of people that you want to belong with, but also a group that you contribute towards and then do many things together to make it grow and flourish. That one can spread their wings in a foreign land and achieve their dreams, but when evening comes close and the birds are returning home you need your own kith and kin to unwind, talk, eat, laugh and support before the great wirepuller up there instructs "PACK UP."

■

SECTION 2:

A Life in Pictures

Visit to France

Mayfair Hotel, Puri

At Taj Mahal, Agra, India

MayFair, Puri

With first car

At her in laws kitchen, Cuttack

Buckingham Palace, London

Historic place in India

Visit to France

Gardening in 14 Champlain Way residence

Historic place in India

In her kitchen

At work place

At Long Island residence, NYC

Champu Chhanda

after wedding

At a function

At Ctc residence

A lake in New York

At Banaras

Wedding

Servants of India Society - Cuttack house

Servants of India Society - Cuttack house

NYC - Brookyln

May Fair Hotel, Puri

YOU ARE AWESOME

Thanks

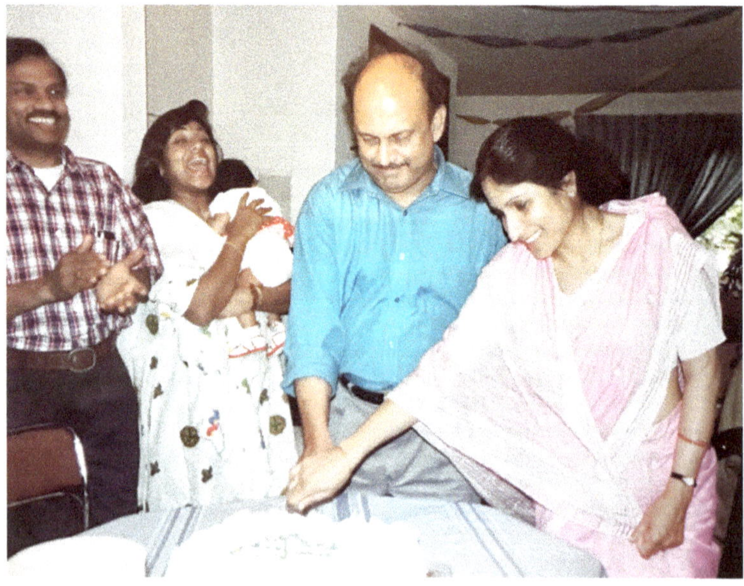

One of her birthday

Bhaina's stepmother's mother

At Taj Mahal, Agra

With her best friend

With the complete in-laws family

With her parents

With her elder sister (extreme left)

With her best friend - Chabi Padhi

With her granny

With Candy Shweder (she who sponsored bhaina's visa)

Servants Society of India, Choudwar

Witth her best friend - Chabi Padhi at Bangkok

SECTION 3:

Lata Nani, we Knew and Loved

A Story of Two Chapters

Chandra Sekhar Singha Babu

In the timeless realm, life is an eternal journey. Time is ruthless. Lata Apa started a new eternal journey leaving behind Sashi Bhaina. Lata Apa got admitted to the hospital with a serious illness. Each passing day dwindled hopes of survival then kindled back with a new lease of life. I'm trying to be a face reader of Sashi Bhaina on the way back from hospital to home.

Before I asked my usual question "How is Lata Apa doing today?"; he surpassed me with a somber shattered voice "Lata is through her last days".

His despaired looks - was looking beyond the front car shield. I felt a deep vacuum. Just yesterday we had been discussing renewed hope after the successful surgery. A food pipe bypassing the esophagus was inserted into the abdomen, connecting directly to the stomach to deliver necessary nutrients to live. I was wondering what the worth of living is.

Lata Apa will never eat again - will never taste food again. Even a little drink to moist her throat may cause pneumonia by pulmonary aspiration. The thought made me awake as a philosopher. Who says we live for food? Perhaps they had to explore many dimensions of life. I know Lata Apa is a food lover. Rather I say she had a great sense of taste for food. She was a great cook. I relished many dishes on pre and post sickness days. Countless times she stood up to cook for me. Her unsteady body with the help of an unstable walker got ready to prepare many recipes with love. Sometimes I win to prevent her. Sometimes not. She was invincible.

I reflected on my word "invincible". Does it exaggerate?

I reflect on my disarrayed thoughts. Never and ever, I heard from Lata Apa that she would like to die. Never expressed her wish to die to avoid any suffering. She had a lively life, a love for life. Love for Bhaina. Perhaps it was the oasis of her inner strength to fight against her illness. Although many thoughts plagued her in her last days. How could she depart from her life partner? Who will take care of Bhaina in her absence?

She endured all pain and fought for life until Bhaina released her.

"Go Lata, go. Today is a very auspicious day." Bhaina was getting ready to say farewell. He knew that he would never fly ever with one wing. As if Lata Apa was waiting for this bidding time. Her fag-end of life ended up in a thin air. No pain and no suffering. I was differentiating, suffering from pain. In the last three-four years Lata Apa visited many times in urgent care, was hospitalized, and then returned home triumphant as if she was returning from a war.

I always found her stable in mind while her feet disarrayed with dwindling strength. She was a courageous woman and truly a fighter.

Very few people used to call on our land line and Lata Apa was one of them. She had a very sharp voice.

"Call from Lata Misra." a very distinctive announcement over the Caller ID. Charged the inactive air in the home for a quick response.

As a fast responder, I swiftly picked up the receiver to hand over to my wife.

In transition I pray everything must stay well.

No, no, not now. Lata Apa's 50th marriage anniversary is still pending. OSA 50th convention without Lata Apa, Oh, No.

Not now, until this or that is not over. She can't go untimely. She shouldn't.

Lightening of thoughts disappear hearing her bossy voice. "Ae Oh Riti Mohanty, where have you been so long?" A jolt of deep breath with abrupt calm tranquil the raised heart beats.

My wife responds using her best soothing music. "Lata Apa! I was busy with your work. Preparing kids for your next program". I knew it would level down the sentiments restoring back the hurting pride. How can someone forget to call Lata Apa?

"How many kids are participating this time?" questioned Lata Apa.

Their call is very much in the predictable line due to my long-time experience as a passive listener.

Riti replies cautiously. "Lata Apa, some new kids join

this time".

Then the talk quickly entered into a reporting conversation. What they are learning, how old they are and where they belong to, including some information on their parents and their state of preparation. The tempo of conversation goes further, singing a few lines from Lata Apa's favorite song. She must be relieved that you are not derailed from your destination. She was interested in her empire, established in Champu, Chhanda and Odissi and its expansion. She was a heavyweight boxer in the cultural arena.I have seen many punched faces in the straight fight. She was an epitome of our cultural evolution.

So many decades of dedication, participation, contribution, and inspiration to build a cultural heritage to defend, protect, learn and practice our own tradition is a lot to Lata apa's creditable accomplishments.

Lata Apa was a great singer, dramatist, CCO promoter, senior community leader, critic, mentor, advisor, flag bearer and protector of our Odia culture. Truly laudable to her lifetime achievement awarded by OSA. She was a recipient of many awards in her decades of dedication to keep our tradition alive.

Out of many iconic performances, Lata Apa's role in Patent Medicine, Ae Rango Rahile Hela, Kali Jai and many more golden beads to be added to her acclaimed garland. Lata Apa actively participated until the last OSA convention in NJ in 2019. She was the director of Facetime, a NY-NJ chapter drama. Who knew that like Facetime her last rites would be shown in real time over the internet? That was a coincidence to the theme of the drama.

I was tossing fiction over fact. Is life a drama or drama is a life. Introspecting my thoughts. Maybe the latter is correct for Lata Apa.

Last year – feels like yesterday, she called me over the phone. We were all reeling under the midst of a pandemic. We hardly visited each other's home.

Riti handed over the receiver informing me that Lata Apa will talk to me. "Chandra Sekahr Ji" – Lata Apa cracked with her laryngitic voice.

Sometimes she addressed me ending with Ji. I smiled ironically.

"Yes, Lata Apa". She bluntly approached without a plot.

"I can live some more days if you write a drama. Can you write a script on Sanjukta – Prithviraj?"

I thrived with an undenied and undying long-standing request.

Lata Apa's interest in drama was unprecedented. As if it redefines what is called passion. Since then, I have discussed the drama plot a number of times with her. I felt like letting her down when she was no longer renewing her request.

I vividly remember the evening of June 24th, a night before Lata Apa's last marriage anniversary, to celebrate with her. On her deathbed she spoke quietly to Manasi. I asked her, "What Lata Apa transpired to you?" She said, "we will do another drama".

Unbelievable! Almost three weeks before her demise she expressed her interest. Amazing! I was redefining Lata Apa as a great dramatist on a new scale. Has a person like her ever suffered? Silently I nudged my head being unassertive. Unlocking lessons from Lata Apa's life to understand what is called living a life larger than life.

I was sitting across Bhaina in his living room. My privileged uninterrupted time with him. It was around 9 PM. Tonight, in comparison to other days, there were fewer visitors. Regular visitors had already had their sessions with him or maybe now in the temple for Ratha Yatra. Since hospice days not a single day has gone without visitors. Are they visitors or relatives? Drawing a thin line to segregate them in vain. Duma, the caretaker of Lata Apa asked if we would like to have dinner. She muttered that for the last ten days or more she had cooked nothing. I was aware that breakfast, lunch, and dinner were being delivered at home. While silently praying for this love and care to continue, I tried to hold back my emotions over empathy. So much love, affection and affinity reciprocate to pay back with dividends for these two elderly couples. I was becoming a philosopher again. Weighing blood relationships. If blood binds stronger or does love?

Un-intentionally testing the tensile strength of an unbreakable tie created by a couple through love and affection. I was redefining these undefined genres of kith and kin. I chuckled at my own wits.

"No, we had dinner already," Riti answered Duma.

It was the first time she visited Lata Apa's home without Lata Apa. Visibly it was different. The same home, same furniture, same lights and perhaps the same brightness, but feeling no energy. A dejected feeling engulfed the whole house. I was comparing home to a living body without a soul. I was wondering if it was time to go to bed for Sashi Bhaina. I noticed Bhaina's left palm rolled over his forehead unwittingly when he felt either sleepy or in a state of dilemma.

I came to my feet. "Bhaina it's time to go to bed."

He appealed abruptly, "sit for a while."

"No Bhaina, it must be a weary day for you." We left while Doma was closing the door behind us. Had a cursory look at the marigolds blooming with many buds at the front entrance. I planted them on Mother's Day. Exhaled with a deep compression from my heart as if it was my last deedd for Lata Apa. She will not request to plant here after.

I shifted to reverse gear. Traversing back with increased distance, I was feeling apart from a motherly love. Consoling myself that it is the end of chapter one - of a story of two chapters.

■

Plainsboro, New Jersey

In Loving Memory of Lata Nani

Pradeep Mohapatra

"First impressions last long". This is how Lata Nani came into my life. It was the evening of Thanksgiving dinner at my uncle's house in the state of Maryland and my first in the USA. Her commanding voice and dignified style was standing out in the crowd. The few minutes I spent with her during my introduction was enough for me to realize that she was someone special. Fast forward a few years, I ended up being part of her iconic stage drama "Patent Medicine" where she left no stone unturned to awe the audience with her heart touching performance. Who knew our cultural journey together would pick up speed on the OSA platform creating many memories until ......

In loving memory of our dearest Lata Nani, it is hard to put into words the depth of our loss and the immense void her absence has left in our society. She was not just a beloved OSA member but a guiding light, a source of inspiration, and a pillar of strength for all of us. Her unwavering love for the community and kindness touched everyone she met, and her smile had the power to brighten even the gloomiest days. Lata nani had a deep-rooted passion for Odia culture, and her involvement in OSA cultural performances was nothing short of extraordinary.

Whether it was her artistic presentation of stage drama, her melodious voice in classical songs, or her meticulous attention to detail in organizing cultural events, she embodied the essence of our rich heritage. Living in a foreign land, she was deeply committed to preserving our native language "Odia", often organizing language classes and local radio programs to ensure the younger generation stayed connected to their linguistic roots.

She had an incredible eye for artistic talent and was always the first to appreciate and encourage the skills of young performers within our Odia community. She identified their potential by observing their abilities in areas such as dance, singing, and art. Once she recognized their talents, she nurtured them by offering encouragement and motivation, creating opportunities for them to showcase their skills during and outside many OSA events. She fostered a supportive environment where young performers felt confident to step out of their comfort zones and express themselves. Her efforts not only helped many young adults grow with amazing cultural values but also instilled a sense of pride and belonging within the community.

Lata Nani had a unique ability to motivate members of the community to step out of their comfort zones and showcase their talents, fostering a sense of pride and belonging among everyone. She taught us the importance of Odia language, music & dance art by our community members irrespective of the age groups to stay connected to our roots and instilled in us a sense of pride in our traditions. Her dedication and enthusiasm were unmatched, and she always encouraged us to participate, learn, and celebrate our culture with the same passion. We are forever grateful for the countless memories she had created the lessons she conveyed, and the love she showered upon us.

Though she is no longer with us, her spirit will continue to live on in the rhythms of the stage drama she performed, the songs she sang, the language she preserved, and the values she upheld. She created a vibrant cultural environment that strengthened the community's connection to its roots, even in a foreign land. Her legacy of promoting artistic expression and cultural pride continues to influence and shape the community's identity, ensuring that their traditions remain alive and cherished for years to come.

My Dear Lata Nani, you will always be remembered in our heart with love and gratitude.

■

Lata Nani: A Personal Tribute to a Cultural Guardian

Lalatendu Mohanty

Some people come into our lives quietly, without much noise. Others arrive with such a strong presence that they change everything forever. Lata Nani was the second type—a powerful woman who touched everyone she met. My story with her wasn't simple; it was full of respect and fights, arguments and make up, and finally, deep love.

When We First Met

It was 2009. I was at my first convention as chapter president, full of new ideas and excitement. I had seen how talented our young people were and wanted to give them a chance to shine.

But there was already someone important in the cultural world—Lata Nani. She wasn't just a volunteer; she was a legend. For years, she had shaped our conventions with her ideas, her hard work, and her love for Odia art.

My plan seemed fair: to bring in fresh ideas while asking her to be an advisor. But I didn't understand who she really was. Lata Nani wasn't made to sit in the background. She was a leader, not someone who just watched. When she learned our plan, she decided not to attend the convention at all.

I was shocked and upset. People around me whispered, "She can be stubborn... she can even be mean." For a while, I believed them.

The Day Everything Changed

But life gave us another chance. A few of us decided to visit her at home—we said we were "just passing by" and wanted to stop for tea. It was my first time in her house, and I wasn't sure what would happen.

What came next surprised me. We didn't talk about culture, programs, or leadership. Not one word about conventions. Instead, we just had a normal visit—hot tea, easy conversation, and quiet reminders of how important she was to us.

That's when I first saw her soft side, a gentleness she didn't show easily. From that moment came her new dream: to teach Odia classical music to the next generation.

Her Dream Comes True

Soon after, Lata Nani began putting all her energy into something bigger than any single convention. She dreamed of creating a place for Odia classical music in America, and she made it happen.

Her vision created Champu, Chhanda, and Odissi In the history of OSA that year. She supported training, recordings, and performance-planting seeds that will keep Odia culture alive for years to come.

Many times, she made me her "go-to person." Whether it was making the Champu, Chhanda, Odissi Karaoke CD or organizing programs for visiting artists, she trusted me and believed in me. Each time she did this, it didn't just give me work to do—it gave me confidence. Her trust in me made me a stronger leader and gave me courage to keep serving our community.

Our Many Fights

Of course, it wasn't always easy. Lata Nani and I argued many times. We disagreed about how to do things, we fought about decisions, and there were times when she was angry with me and I pushed back against her.

But in every fight, I knew the truth: she cared deeply. She cared about culture, about keeping things authentic, about doing right by the art forms she loved. And she cared about people, even if she didn't always show it clearly.

I found my own way to break through her tough exterior—a big hug. No matter how tense things got, a hug could always soften the moment and bring back the gentleness she kept hidden from the world.

The Real Person Behind the Legend

That was Lata Nani. Strong-willed, stubborn, sometimes difficult—but also deeply caring, quietly loving, and incredibly generous in spirit. She was more than a cultural leader. She was a protector of our heritage.

She carried the weight of tradition but also the love of family. She wasn't just building programs; she was building a bridge—a way for Odia-Americans to stay connected to their roots, no matter how far they were from Odisha.

Her Lasting Gift

When I look back, what strikes me most isn't the arguments or disagreements, but how she turned her passion into a gift for future generations. She took what could have been a moment of giving up (skipping a convention) and turned it into a life mission—making sure that Odia music and dance would never disappear in America.

To me, she will always be the "stubborn softie"—the woman who fought hard, loved harder, and left us with something priceless.

Her legacy isn't just in performances or programs. It lives in the children who sing Champu with confidence, in the dancers who perform Odissi with pride, and in every hug she gave—hesitant at first, but with her whole heart once she let you in.

Final Thoughts

Lata Nani wasn't perfect. None of us are. But she was real. She was passionate. And she was ours.

Her legacy will outlast all of us, written not in stone but in music, rhythm, and community. For me, she was not only an icon but also family. I will always carry the memory of her stubbornness, her trust, her dreams, and her hidden tenderness in my heart.

That was Lata Nani. And we are all better because she was part of our journey.

■

OSA President 2018-19
New Jersey

Lata Mishra, I knew

Chabi Padhi

My name is Chhabi Padhi. I met Lata nani for the first time when I was living in Connecticut in 1981. We were not sisters by blood; we were soul sisters. From that day until her last day we had a close relationship even though I was living in California and she was in New Jersey.

How do I describe her in a few words?

She was beautiful from inside to outside. She was not only my sister, but she was also a mentor to me too. When I was in Connecticut there was an Oriya Convention in New Jersey. As all who knew her must know how passionate she was about Oriya drama. She asked me to participate in the drama. I was not comfortable acting in front of so many people. She encouraged me with her strong voice.

"Chhabi, you can do it."

She can't take no for an answer. So, I did participate and I enjoyed it thoroughly. We went on vacation together a couple of times. Our first trip together was to Maui in 1984. We were driving in Maui and saw so many mango trees full of colorful mangoes. She asked my husband "you must stop the car. We must pick some of these mangoes.

No one is here so we can reach the branch and get them." She was so excited we had to stop and picked at least 10 pounds of them and brought them to hotel. She packed all of them in a duffel bag. So thrilled she could enjoy them at home.

The next day we were at the airport and at the inspection area they said we can't take any fruits to the mainland and dumped all those beautiful mangoes. You should have seen her face. It was priceless. I will never forget that. One of the funny moments I remember was another Oriya convention in Newport Beach CA. Lots of oriya people knew her but not me. I was going in the elevator. One Oriya gentleman said Lata Apa, "I just saw you in the lobby. How did you come here so fast? I told him I'm not Lata Apa. He was surprised. When I told Lata nani we laughed so much. In the end I can only say her beaming personality taught me to live, laugh and love. That's something I will never lose. The memories we shared will never be forgotten . I'm a better person to have such a wonderful friend and sister.

■

Lata Mishra, as I remember her

Jnana Ranjan Dash

I met Lata Mishra for the first time in the spring of 1975, although I had met Sashi Babu three years before during my first trip to New York from Canada. The couple had come to Toronto in 1975 with a guest and stayed at my place. I started calling her Lata Bhabi. She and Sashi Babu knew my wife's family quite well from Cuttack. As Sashi Babu was related to my wife's grandmother (Late Padmabhusan Sri Radhanath Rath's wife, Sabitri Devi), she always recollected the love and affection of Mrs. Rath from the time of her wedding to Sashi Babu. Lata Bhabi loved my wife Bui from the first time she saw her.

I remember the time we stayed at their apartment in Queens during the bicentennial celebration in 1976. In the following decades we met numerous times at their homes in Little Neck, Dix Hills, and New Jersey. I had taken my parents and my in-laws to their Little Neck house back in 1982 and 1987. During my months of commuting to Armonk (IBM Headquarters) in 1991, I would stop by in Dix Hills to have Lata Bhabi's delicious home-cooked dinner and then drive to White Plains. Their house was like The Utkal Bhavan swarming with guests and visitors. I used to joke that Sashi babu provided a taxi service to pick up (and drop off) guests at JFK. Both of them were like magnets drawing people to their home all the time. The husband-wife duo were magnificent hosts.

Both had been to our home in California a few times, specially to attend the wedding of both my sons in 2009 and 2012. The last time we were together was during the OSA Convention in 2019 when I drove them to Atlantic City and we stayed with them for a couple of days before and after the event. She was unwell then and needed a wheelchair to move around.

During the last few years of her life, she insisted on joining me for morning meditation and Satsang. She was an intent listener and found inner peace during those sessions. Although her physical body was failing, she started to realize the essence of the Sat-Chit-Ananda Atma (eternal and deathless) that defined her real identity. Every time we finished our Satsang, a smile returned to her face. I saw pure Ananda in that smile. She never complained about her health. Her attitude to bear the physical pain and rise above it was remarkable. She proved the dictum, "pain is compulsory, but suffering is optional".

We often talked about the music of Odisha. She sang beautifully those Odishi songs like "Sahiba Ki E Nishi Go, Nagara Mohan Bina", a Sikandar Alam special. Her keen interest in the traditional Odishi music like Chhaanda and Champu culminated in a regular OSA Convention event named after her. Her effort to infuse Odia classical music in children was unique. She acted well in dramas such as "Patent Medicine", staged during OSA Conventions in New Jersey and Dallas.

Lata bhabi enjoyed a good story or narration of an event and was an eager listener.

During our elder son's wedding at a California winery, she came and told me "Jnana Babu, I just saw a lady who resembles so much with the top Bengali actress Rituparna Ghosh."

I said, "Actually you saw the real actress Rituparna who is here with her husband Sanjay, a friend of mine."

With dilated eyes, she rushed to meet Rituparna and get her autograph. What a child-like innocence! Another time in 1987, I had gone to NY to receive my sister Rina who was arriving for the first time from India after marriage. We came to their home in Dix Hills (Long Island). Sashi Babu was in Chicago and due to bad weather; he was stuck there. Lata Bhabi alone took full care of my newly arrived sister, making her feel like she was still in Odisha. Her care and kindness always stood out. The inner virtues of goodness-of-heart and spreading love was the hallmark of Lata Mishra's character.

Our scriptures say that when the physical body drops, the subtle body (mind and the indriyas) continues the journey, just like a wind carries the fragrance of a flower (Vayur Gandha Nibasayet – Ch.15, Gita). The flower is the body which remains behind, but the fragrance is carried by the Jeevatma.

Lata Mishra's fragrant personality lives forever in our hearts. now, when I do namaskar to her, I can see her smiling face joyfully greeting me in her house.

■

San Jose, California

Lata Nani , A Nightingale

Pratap Das

I came to the USA in 1973 to Washington DC and have settled there ever since. In those days, there were only a few Odia families in the New York/New Jersey/ Connecticut, Washington DC and New England areas. They had just built a small social organization under the leadership of late Dr. Krushna Mohan Das, Late Dr. Amiya Patnaik called the New York Odias. Even though there were another 100 families scattered throughout the United States, the Odisha Society of America (OSA) was not formed officially.

There was no concept of having a convention till 1974. It was just a mere Odia get together for an afternoon, with a small General Body meeting, a small limited cultural program by the attendees followed by a home cooked dinner. About 20-30 people used to attend. This was done during the Labor Day weekend and people living in their friend's houses. It was 1975, and 1976 it was held at a small church at River Vale, NJ close to Dr. Amiya Patnaik's house. In 1977, it was held at Rutgers University.

I arrived at Sashibhaina's apartment in New York city, where I met Lata Nani for the first time. I never knew that she was a singer. I was singing and playing tabla in

Ravenshaw College and Vani Vihar in the late 60s and early part of the 70s before I left for the USA. My association with Akshya Mohanty and Sikander Alam was noticed by both Sashibhaina and Lata Nani. As we all know, Late Sikander Alam was a close friend of Sashibhai from Cuttack. Lata Nani and I were introduced and the chemistry worked – we started performing at the OSA conventions, Kumar Purnima programs and many occasions.

I am not an expert in Odia traditional vocal music, but I have heard hundreds of singers singing Odissi, Chanda, and Champu. But there is something with the timber of her voice. It was lilting and melodious, typically Odissi. Very few singers such as Late Balakrishna Das, Shyamamani Patnaik, Ramahari Das, Sangeeta Gosain, Nazia Alam, Bijoy Jena etc. have rendered songs in a way it should be sung and heard. God had given her the blessings to render the songs to make us proud. I always adored her tone and presentations.

Slowly Lata Nani became a prominent singer at any Odia programs with her Odissi, Chanda and Champu. Not only was she a singer but also started promoting Odissi, Chanda, and Champu in North America. She became a pioneer in inspiring the children to learn the music and advising the parents to encourage their children learning Odissi vocal. She convinced the OSA Executives to make such traditional authentic Odia music renditions as a part of the OSA activities. She visioned that contemporary Hindi and modern Odia music is almost damaging the Odia culture and Odia musical traditions.

Eventually, OSA Executives decided to name the Odissi, Chanda & Champu after her.

Personally, Lata Nani managed all the Odissi, Chanda, & Champu sessions with a competition to keep up the quality. I saw every year the entries were getting higher and parents were preparing their kids to perform well. To see such a revolution of introducing the lilting melody of traditional Odia music born in North America. What an accomplishment! Today, when we hear any Odia kid rendering an Odissi – it reminds us about the person behind this saga.

Lata Nani was a pioneer and wanted to make it easier for the kids to learn with full accompaniment by producing tracks of popular Odissi, Chanda & Champu songs. Lata Nani realized that the students are lacking percussionists (Mardala) and the music. Artists like Dr. Sangeeta Gosain and Dr. Nazia Alam assisted Lata Nani producing several tracks. Several kids benefitted to learning the lyrics and the tune. Tears came to my eyes and my heart was filled with joy about how Lata Nani inspired Odia traditional music to American Odia kids.

Later, we met many times talking about the promotions and how to facilitate the process. Singers like Sangeeta Gosain and Nazia Alam visited many chapters of the United States to hold workshops and teach face to face with students. Not only our children were benefitted but also the visiting Odia artists got an opportunity to visit the United States of America.

In the journey of our lives, we meet & greet people and say painful good byes. Our Lata Nani became sick and her health started getting worse. She left us but her inspiration for Odissi, Chanda and Champu is still murmuring in the air. Our memories hunt us but I am so privileged to meet a musical soulmate like Lata Nani.

While mentioning her attributes to Odia vocal music, I must mention that she was also a great stage actor. I still remember "Patent Medicine" by Fakir Mohan Senapati. She performed the character of Sulochana so well with Manaranjan Pattanayak as Chandramanibabu as the Zamindar. Lots of credits go to Sashibhaina to support her efforts and ensure she accomplished her dreams. Many others in New York/New Jersey areas have shown their compassion during her passage. Truly, it takes a village.

I called her the nightingale because her life symbolized love for Odia music and transience of her life. Lata Nani, a selfless simple person with unconditional love is rare. In my journey in the United States of America, I have not found a second one like her. She will be missed on the stage. But she will be in our hearts forever.

■

Remembering Lata Mausi: A Force of Nature

Chandana Pradhan

As I pen these words for this commemorative book, the memory of Lata Mausi remains vivid in our community's collective consciousness. Though time has passed since her departure, her presence still echoes in our gatherings and cultural events.

From our first meeting, Lata Mausi defied expectations. Learning of my family connections, she immediately took us under her wing, insisting we call her 'Mausi.' This instant warmth, juxtaposed with her reputation for a fiery temper, was my first glimpse into her multifaceted personality.

Mausi and her husband had a playful side that never failed to bring smiles. They christened my tall husband with a Bollywood star's name, a nickname that stuck. Even now, it warms our hearts to hear Mausi's husband use that name, a cherished reminder of the bond we share and the joy Mausi brought into our lives.

Mausi's passion for our culture was legendary, particularly evident in her stage performances. Her portrayal in the "Patent Medicine" show is still talked about today, a testament to her theatrical prowess and the lasting impact she had on our community's cultural life. She approached these performances with an intensity that could rival professional actors, turning simple community plays into unforgettable experiences.

It's true that Mausi had a quick temper, and she wasn't one to hide her feelings, even in public. Yet, paradoxically, this same intensity made her love and affection all the more powerful when bestowed. She had a special fondness for my dhokla, a small detail that became a touching symbol of our connection.

Her relationship with her husband was as complex as she was. Their dynamic bond, with its ups and downs, was a part of who they were as a couple. Despite occasional public disagreements, their enduring partnership was a cornerstone of our community.

Lata Mausi's later years taught us valuable lessons about resilience and the importance of community. Even as her health declined, her spirit remained strong. She continued to attend functions, always elegantly dressed, her presence a reminder of her unwavering commitment to our cultural heritage.

As we contribute to this book of memories, let's celebrate Lata Mausi in all her complexity. She taught us that it's possible to be both feared and loved, to be a force for tradition and a catalyst for bringing people together. Her legacy lives on in the cultural programs she championed, the friendships she forged, and the community she helped shape.

We remember Lata Mausi not just for her temper or

her theatrical talents, but for the totality of who she was - a passionate defender of our traditions, a fierce friend, and a woman who loved deeply, even if she didn't always show it in conventional ways.

■

New Jersey

Our Lata

Shanti Mishra

If Lata had stayed in her village in Odisha, and I had stayed in mine, we might never have crossed paths. But destiny brought us both to America within months in 1972. She came to join her husband Saradindu. I came as a graduate student, alone and unsure. My husband Uma joined me later that year. By chance — or maybe by fate — Lata and I found each other, and our friendship began.

Those early years were not easy. We were young Odia women, far from home, learning to make sense of a strange country. Lata and I leaned on each other, as sisters do. Our bond with Lata and Saradindu only grew stronger. Coincidentally, her village was close to my in-laws' back in Odisha, so even in this faraway land, we carried a thread of familiarity.

When Uma started his residency at Sloan Kettering in Manhattan in 1978, we moved closer. Lata and Saradindu's little apartment in Rego Park became our "adda" spot. Everyone knew their door was always open. We would arrive with sleeping bags, cook together, and talk until midnight. Later, when they moved to Little Neck, weekends at their home became celebrations — more space, more food, more music, more family.

Unlike many Odia women before us, neither of us were content to just stay in the background. We spoke our minds, often too loudly for some people's comfort! When Sikandar Alam toured the U.S. in 1983, we spent that summer together, organizing, cooking, dancing, making things happen. I became good at finding venues, Jayanti managed the money, and Lata took charge of logistics and entertainment. She had indomitable energy packed into one small frame.

When our chapter hosted the 15th OSA Convention at Glassboro State College, Lata poured her heart into the cultural program. I still remember her pride when the children staged the Ramayan. That moment sparked her dream — to teach Odia children songs, Chhanda, Champu, and Odissi, so they would never lose touch with our culture.

That dream became her mission. With her persistence (and Lata could *never* be said "no" to), she brought in talented teachers like Nazia and Riti. She made sure children sang in conventions, not just in our homes. What started as her vision soon became a national movement within OSA. She gave our kids a way to stay Odia in spirit, even if they grew up thousands of miles from Odisha.

But Lata was more than her mission. She had warmth, humor, and style. Her fish curry was famous. Her jokes could make you double over. And she wore sarees with such elegance that we always had to give her extra time before leaving the house. She was full of life, with a softness beneath her occasional stubbornness.

Lata was also the one who pushed boundaries. She, Jayanti, and I were the first women to demand seats at the planning table for OSA events. People criticized us – but we knew we had as much to give as the men. And we did. Together, we helped shape OSA into what it is today.

Her last years were not easy. When the illness came, her voice and body slowly betrayed her. It hurt to see her fade, but her spirit never left. On July 11, 2021, when we were just a mile from her home, the news came that she was gone. My heart broke that day.

I lost a friend, a sister, a partner in mischief and dreams. OSA lost one of its brightest flames. But her legacy lives on in every child who sings Champu, in every Odissi step taken on stage, in every convention where women now sit at the table as equals.

For me, Lata will always be the laughter in my kitchen, the elegance in a saree, the warmth of fish curry on a Sunday, and the determination of a woman who refused to take "no" for an answer. She was family. I miss her deeply, but I smile knowing she is probably organizing a concert in heaven, and telling Bijoy Mahapatra, Kashinath Sahoo, Sikandar Alam and Prafulla Padhi exactly what to do.

■

Lata Misra – My Offerings

Gopal Mohanty

Who could she be in Chitrangada's role in Kabichandra Kali Charan Patnaik's drama 'Chakri'? It was staged during the half-a-day 1980 OSA Convention in the Detroit area. Indeed, the idea was daring in those days. It was almost beyond anyone's imagination when practically everyone having an overload of back-home sentiment, came to attach with each other within that short period and to have a 'ho-ho' time. Of course, OSA was lucky to have Lata Misra and Pramod Patnaik in that event to initiate a process of cultural enrichment by acting extempore as Chitrangada and Arjuna. Coincidentally Bishnu Joshi who was present reciting Srikrushna's lines without any interruption became the obvious choice for Srikrushna's role. For Babrubahana's role Amiya Mohanty was dragged in. The decision was to present a few short pieces from the book. Just then I was attracted to their conversation and no wonder I joined them to set the male characters ready and become the prompter as well as suggesting movements on the stage. Wow! The show went through with unexpected excitement and applause.

Wow! Lata, that daring Odia housewife to be on

stage and that too without any rehearsal and preparation!! Hum!!!

We used to visit my wife Shanti's cousin Bimu Bhai (Bimal Krushna Mahanti) who was working in IBM and living close to his office situated in Westchester County. During his regular family visits to Krushna Babu's (Dr. Krushna Mohan Das) family, living in Queens, New York City, we happened to join whenever we were there. There, very likely I met Saradindu (Misra) Babu, Lata's husband. My attention was primarily focused on Krushna Babu and his wife Basi Apa. Perhaps I might have met Lata there.

Very quickly I learnt that Krushna Babu's place acted as a welcome house for Odias, invariably so to those entering America. His wife, popularly known as 'Basi Apa', was a motherly loving person, practically busy in the kitchen all the time.

It was a matter of time that Lata was known to be the only person who could sing traditional Odia songs like *Odissi, Champu, Chhanda.* I always have a strong passion for Odisha's cultural heritage. So, I got excited when I came to know this. I was unable to recall how she looked like if I saw her but chuckled imagining her singing 'galani ta gala kathare sangata...' or ' kadamba bane banshi...' or or...never mind, anyone that would take me back to the dust and soil of my birthplace.

Incidentally, in the 1984 Convention at Glassboro, NJ, Lata produced and staged Fakir Mohan's 'Patent Medicine' story with youths. For some reason, she wanted me to help her in stage preparation and acting, possibly observing my interest in drama at the 1980 Detroit Convention.

I believe Lata's persistent thought on 'Patent Medicine' became so deep that from Chitrangada, a woman of chastity and purity in Mahabharata, she appeared as Srimati Samarjani (the title used by the eminent dramatist Gopal Chotray) by playing the role of Sulochana Dei in the story, presented at the 2003 OSA Convention held at Princeton. Ha, ha, ha, that was Lata. Through her acting, was she trying to teach all men including Mana Ranjan Babu playing the role of Chandramani Babu, Sulochana's husband and Saradindu Babu, the Convener to treat the wives justly?

For the 1986 Convention in Canada, it was decided to celebrate the 50th anniversary of Odisha as a province/ state. Ashok Babu, the Convener asked me to prepare a plan. Not feeling comfortable with the ceremonial speeches, I thought of using Mayadhar Mansingh's book, 'The Saga of the Land of Jagannatha' in a stage function representing glories and rich culture of Odisha, performed in a unique way by members inclusively spread all over NA, by using various forms of performing arts, music, dance, recitation, drama. Here Lata's exclusive talent in drama and traditional music became most valuable assets in the presentation which continued for three hours.

In the 1994 Convention at Pomona, NJ to celebrate OSA's 25th anniversary, we had a stage performance of the classic novel 'Chhamana Athaguntha' successfully under Lata's blessing. A mutual rapport between the two of us progressed well. It seemed both were infected by the 'drama' bug with no hope of any cure.Lata's bug made her ecstatically imbued by presenting her drama at 2008 Convention. It was staged at the historic and most impressive Patriots Theater in Trenton, NJ.

In the meantime, Lata developed challenging health issues. Yet her inherent artistic qualities had determined propelling force to ride over anything and everything. Yes, her intent love for Odia traditional songs set a momentum to establish in her name, a competition of *Odissi, Champu, Chhanda* in OSA Conventions. It was an unbelievable act in a foreign land.

Was it then a reflection of the unassuming but deep-in-heart Odia spirit that witnessed the establishment of Odisha as the first linguistic province/state in India despite Odia speaking population numerically not being significant, the classical recognition of Odissi despite vehement opposition from the South and of Odia language despite powerful antagonistic scrutinizing eyes of others. And of course, OSA as a socio-cultural organization with a thin numerical base came into existence earlier than other dominating groups from India.

One day in 2014 I received a call from Lata asking me to write a script for Fakir Mohan's short story 'Rebati' in a way so that she could play 'Jejima's role. Despite her deteriorating health condition, she was dreaming of being on stage as if it was her home and life and as if she was a lifelong dreamer. I did send her one, but alas, she could not be on stage although the drama was enacted.

Life's strange twists can be miracles. One of them was our never thought of meeting at an unusual place like

Bhubaneswar Golf Club in 2019. It was related to the 50th anniversary of the OSA Convention organized by the New York/ New Jersey Chapter. We were part of a conversational meeting of OSA seniors present there during early 2019. Participants were: Bhabagrahi Mishra and his wife Shanti (Bhubaneswar), Kalpataru Kanungo (Bhubaneswar), Saradindu and Lata Misra, Birendra Patnaik, Mana Ranjan and Minati Pattanayak, Lalu Mansinha and Charu Hota, Hara and Sumitra Padhi, and myself with my wife Shanti. The afternoon brought a joy of unknown kind from that unassumed event.

Life is a continuity of eventualities. Things happen unknowingly as my relationship with Lata. I offer my gratitude and love to Lata.

■

Lata Nani- Strength and Compassion Within

Jagannath Mohanty

It was early spring, almost the end of winter 2021, late March but in the middle of COVID pandemic. We have all been confined to home for almost a year with all sorts of lockdown and restrictions. With a year of no mobility, no movement, but constant sitting, part of my body showed signs of deterioration manifesting in increasing dull pain on my lower right calf. I had this pain for many years but on and off and I lived with it. But this time it was different, and I had to do something about it.

With multiple consultations with specialists and surgeons, they decided to undergo spinal surgery to relieve the nerve pinching and alleviate the pain.This was around 4 months prior to Lata Nani's last day on this earth. Her health was deteriorating day by day. Unable to speak clearly or communicate, but mind as sharp as a razor.

She was keeping track of my health, as we all were checking on her frequently. My surgery date was fixed towards the 3rd week of March. After pre-surgical clearance I went through lumbar spinal laminectomy. It was very successful. I came back home from the hospital. Friends and families poured in.

A few days passed by. Then one day a senior gentleman showed up at our door with 2 bags in hand. Of course it was our beloved Sashi Bhaina, who himself wasn't doing well. He said "Jagannath, Lata tuma paein pathaichhi tumara favourite Matchha Tarkari. Tume keta bada surgery dei jaichha, khaiba nihati darakar. Khaa aau jaldi bhala hoi jaaa."- Needs an English translation here.

Also, Bhaina added "Lata tuma paein bhaari byasta, matte khaali kahuchhi jaaw tikiea jagannath ku dekhi aasa"

This is not the first time she has impressed us with her culinary skills and love for us. From the day I came to this country and there after any chance she gets we will be invited to their Deer Park house in Long Island. We would be sitting in traffic on belt parkway or 495 cursing the traffic for hours. Then upon reaching their house tired, dejected, pressure to go to bathroom. We hear that familiar voice from Bhaina ""Senda, Jagannath gotie beer hau" , followed by Lata Nani's handmade singada and appetizers, Machha Tarkari and not to mention the best rasagolla in the world. Then someone asked us how bad the traffic was. And we say what traffic?

Then back to my original story of Sashi Bhaina showing up with food after a few days of my surgery. Now think about it . At that time Lata Nani was almost fed by a food tube, can't keep her head straight, can't utter a word correctly, can't walk. She will be on the bed and wheelchair. We look into her eyes, and we can feel the emotions - only if her eyes could talk. Her mind is active and still thinking about others, as if, if she regains her strength she can be the young Lata and feed others and entertain others.

It's unthinkable for someone who doesn't know Lata Nani to think why would she, being in such a bad condition, cook food and send food with Sashi Bhaina and think about me?

Well, I wasn't surprised.

I have seen her being tough, and sometimes vocal with emotions that you don't want to hear, story for another day.

This time it was pure love and compassion that overcame all her bodily inabilities. Her care for me touched me deeply and I can proudly say that's my Lata Nani and I'm lucky to be part of her life.

There was another incident that is noteworthy. It was around 2015 when she was diagnosed with the neuro condition. She was never afraid and was ready to face it head on. Her life didn't stop. She continued to inspire us to organize Champu Chhanda, dramas, birthdays, anniversaries as life intended to be. As she was consulting various doctors and specialists, she was scheduled to be seen by a Neurologist at Columbia Presbyterian hospital NYC.

Getting her to NYC with her condition was no cakewalk, but she was determined. We drove to the city, knowing Columbia Presbyterian would be a challenge—finding the office, the right floor, even parking—not to mention the amount of walking involved. But she was unfettered. She walked with us through the streets and buildings, up elevators and across floors, all the way to the doctor's office and back again. What was impressive was her attitude, positive, resilient, move forward, no look back. She is no longer with us but her impact on our life will long live as we continue to cherish her life.

■

My Dear Lata Nani

Pitambar Sarangi

It was a cool Saturday morning in 1985, and I was delighted at the prospect of meeting Odia families around New York City. It was Kumar Purnima, celebrated by our community across the area. Only a few weeks earlier I had arrived in New York on a two-year assignment with the State Bank of India—nostalgic as ever, not knowing I would so quickly meet families who would fill the void in my life. One of those families was Lata Nani's. My friend and SBI colleague, Bishnu, had invited me to the celebration, where I was introduced to the late Lata Nani, to Sashi Bhaina, and to many others. With a reserved smile she looked at me, as if trying to decide, in that first glance, whether I was a good person she could trust. When I told her my name, her face warmed, as if she had recognized someone dear. Our conversation was brief; she was busy readying the Odia children for the cultural programs—such a thoughtful effort to root those born here in the Odia language, culture, and rituals. The cultural program was wonderful; the children performed beautifully under her direction. We ended the evening with sumptuous Odia food prepared by volunteers—it is worth mentioning Basi Apaa's dalma. I exchanged my phone number and left the venue, and soon after, Lata Nani invited Bishnu and me to visit their home in Little Neck.

On one of the following weekends after work, Bishnu and I boarded a bus to Little Neck. It was a bit dark when we arrived. Sashi Bhaina and Lata Nani welcomed us with evening snacks. From the kitchen she called out, "Pitambar, you know I am also a Sarangi." At that moment I understood her expression from the other day. From then on she treated me as her younger brother. Between 1985 and 1988 I visited Lata Nani and Sashi Bhaina many times. In the meantime, they moved from Little Neck to Dix Hills (Long Island). When they came to Flushing for Indian groceries, Lata Nani would ask me to join them. She made wonderfully tasty food—her Sajana Chhuin sorisa (drumsticks in mustard sauce), one of my favorites, was out of this world. Every time I visited, she prepared it for me. When my tenure at SBI ended, I was expected to return to India, but the love, affection, and steady support from Sashi Bhaina and Lata Nani played a role in my decision to come back to the USA and reshape my future.

Later, when they moved to Monmouth Junction, New Jersey, and then to South Brunswick, she made sure I performed the Griha Pravesh pujas. I am not a traditionally trained priest, but she had enormous trust in me. Any small thing I did for her or for Sashi Bhaina made me feel very good. Having them in this land, far away from home, eased the absence of my own sister and brother-in-law.

At the 2005 OSA convention, where Sashi Bhaina

served as convener, Lata Nani oversaw the cultural programs. She wanted to ensure that local talent was well represented, with a few artists from Odisha. By no means was I a singer, but because of her I made my singing debut in the opening ceremony. I believe I got that chance because she loved me like a younger brother. What kindness. As hosts, Lata Nani and Sashi Bhaina were unparalleled. Many artists from Odisha, when they toured the USA, stayed with them and felt at home.

Lata Nani was soft-spoken, kind-hearted, and deeply empathetic. A true lover of Odia culture, she poured herself into keeping our language, music, and Odissi dance alive in America. She was diligent to the point of perfection—program sheets marked in pencil, costume boxes neatly labeled, rehearsals repeated until every step and mudra felt just right. Through her single-minded effort, Chhanda and Champu, which had nearly faded even back home, became a permanent fixture at OSA conventions.

Life was not easy for her toward the end. A neurological illness arrived quietly and would not let go. It pained me to see her struggle to eat and to watch the illness gain ground, day by day. Yet whenever I visited, she would wave me to a chair and turn to the stove— "Just a minute," she'd say—insisting on cooking something simple and comforting, the way she always had. She kept doing that until she became bedridden. Through it all, her first questions were always about me: Was I eating well? How was my health? And what about Kunmun's marriage? The illness overpowered her body, but it never dimmed her kindness.

A day or two before her passing, a few of us decided to gather at her bedside and recite chapters from the Bhagavad Gita. I arrived on time, but grief overwhelmed me, and I could not recite even a shloka. Knowing her, I think she would have wanted me to chant, and I regret that I could not. My dear Lata Nani, please forgive me. My pranam to you, wherever you are.

■

Remembering Lata Maushi

Sagarika Mishra

ଫୁଲଣ ଦେବୀକୁ ଆଣିଛୁ କି ?

Reverberated with a nudge like a sweet motherly fond tripping down from my memory lane.

Alas! Time! I was opening the past in my present.

Lata Mausi gone. Left a vacuum to be filled with emptiness. Holding a part of the door wide open and looking at the big picture frame on the wall.

As if winking at me from the depth of slumbered eyes inquesting in her usual authoritarian style.

ଗୋଟିଏ ମାସ ହେଲାଣି କଉଠି ଥିଲୁ ?

I was filled with a nostalgic pain. Impulsed through a subconscious mind oozing out from an embankment of emotion.

ମୋ ଝିଅ ଫୁଲଣଦେବୀ କାହିଁକି ହେବ ବା ? ଖୋଜୁ ଥିଲେ ଯଦି ଫୋନ କରି ଡାକିଲେନି ?

Throttled out the emotive flow. A special bondage dried up at the demise of Mausi. My daughter and son who were blessed with grandparental (ଅଜା-ଆଈ) love and attachment, also lost the affinity.

I found Mausa sitting on a chair, it felt like a broken rhythm and his melodious voice sounds to me like a melancholy song. My daughter was bending upon his feet for blessing.

Mausi belonged to the same maternal village Narisho in Nialli giving me a special empowerment in her home. I was enjoying special privileges and overridden by special rights too. She calls me for domestic help unhesitantly. Specifically, taking care of her plants, believing in my green thumb.

Taking advantage, I took out jasmine saplings and later gave one to Chandra Bhai. Now offspring of the same jasmine species spread through the community. But the original plant that was more than 35 years old did not survive at Mausi's home. Perhaps the plant lost to her mother and lost the interest to live in. Very sad.

On many occasions I prepare Dalima for Mausa on demand from Mausi. She praised my kitchen garden while visiting my home on many special days. Mausa was a blissful breeze for his charming personality.

In contrast, Mausi was a task master and perfectionist. I feel her as a coconut at top but soft inside like a mother to her baby. It was more revealing while in the drama rehearsals.

Mausi was best known as a dramatist.

Years back, I was playing the lead role - Rebati in Rebati, the iconic odia drama. Needless to say it was based on a legendary odia novelist Fakir Mohan Senapati. The pivotal character, Rebati was a young innocent village girl of the then 18th century and I had to play the role.

Lata Mausi was the director and already earned a lot of respect within the Odia community for her acting and directing skills.

On the day of the final show I put on lipsticks in my makeup as a village girl. I thought it would be a trivial matter to be noticed but I have been criticized till day.

On top of my silly mistake, another fun thing happens when Bapi Bhai continues to focus the spotlight on Bijoy who played in my opposite and had to die on stage.

He was supposed not to wake up until the lights went off. But how long can he pretend to be dead on stage? So a dead man wakes up to say to turn off the spotlight. A sad scene evokes uncontrollable humor for us when and when we recollect the play.

Mausi has gone but her sweet rebuke for using lipstick still echoing in the ear.

ଆଲୋ ଜବିରୀ, ତୁ ହେଲୁ ପରା ସେ କାଳର ଗାଁ ଝିଅ, କିଏ କହିଲା ଓଠ ଲାଲ କରିବା ପାଇଁ ? ଲିପ୍‌ଷ୍ଟିକ ପାଇଲୁ କଉଠୁ ?

Chandra Bhai came out to defend me.

ଲତା ଅପା ! ଗାଁ ଝିଅ ହେଲା ବୋଲି ପୋଇ ମଞ୍ଜି ବି ପାଇବ ନାହିଁ।

The fun dragged deeper than defending me. But it still tenders as a sweet admittance to my wits.

Then came Face-Time. A tragic drama story tries to bring out the helpless side of individuals living thousands miles away from the country.

A fictitious but factual unfortunate incident occurred in the life of NRIs to be played for OSA convention 2019 in Atlantic city, New Jersey. I played a supernatural role as "Niyati". Again, as a director we had enough scope to learn acting from Mausi. We had a very good time with Mausa and Mausi together in all rehearsals.

I miss Lata Mausi, who was a family member to me. I owe my gratitude to Mausa and Mausi who helped me during my difficult time as my local guardians. Lata Mausi can't override Niyati's script or direction. Finally, Niyati had her last laugh.

■

Plainsboro, New Jersey

Late Lata Mishra—A Living Legacy

Niranjan Pati

I still remember the summer of 2009, when I first saw Lata Mishra at an OSA convention in New Jersey. The banquet hall that evening brimmed with the familiar comforts of nostalgia—Tabla beats echoing across rented walls, foam plates heavy with *dalma, khatta,* and *mutton curry,* lighthearted banters about the taste of *rasagola* and *chhena poda,* and tongue-in-cheek discussion about the most "bejeweled" women in the crowd. Before that night, I had only heard her name whispered in admiration among Odia diaspora here and dramatists yet meeting her in person revealed something more profound. She was not a performer vying for attention, but a quiet force, making sure everyone else was doing their assigned part. By the time the OSA convention concluded, it was clear to me: I had met someone for whom Odia culture was not an occasional pursuit but the very air she breathed. In her presence, the diaspora did not exude the FOB (fresh out of boat) feeling; it felt like home. To me and my family, she became Lata Nani!

Lata Nani's greatest gift was her stewardship of Odia literary traditions, particularly the delicate art forms of

Chhanda and *Champu*. To many outside Odisha, these may seem like relics in danger of fading, but they echoed her passion when Lata Nani spoke about them. She created Karaoke tracks of these songs so that our younger generation would learn them seriously while having fun. I could remember my daughter Angie reciting *"To lagi Gopa danda ..."* throughout our drive to Chicago to participate in the Chhanda competition at OSA that Lata Nani championed. For diaspora families like ours, juggling Kumon math classes and soccer practices while trying to pass along a few words of Odia to our children, she was a breathing bridge to heritage. Her message was never about preserving culture as a spectator sport; it was an invitation to be in the thick of it like a participation sport. That was the spirit she carried.

Odia drama was Lata Nani's other grand stage. With a director's keen eye and a sister's stubborn warmth, she coaxed IT professionals, doctors, and accountants, people who had left their youthful flair for drama, into staying up past midnight rehearsing plays like *Kalijai, Patent Medicine,* and even *"Landa Mundia driver"* that her husband, Sashi bhaina enacted. Under her guidance, even a recluse IT professional could turn into a tragic hero on the stage, a modern women professional could become an epitome of tragedy to make the audience weep, and a child with minimal exposure to Odia language could sing fluent Champu and Chhanda. Suburban New Jersey stages could suddenly transform into the temples, villages, and mythic landscapes of Odisha with her directions. For her, living Odia art forms was not about applause but about memory. It reminded us of who we were before we became immigrants, lost in the din and bustle of our lives. That magic was uniquely Lata Nani's.

But she was not only an impresario of words and performances. Lata Nani's hospitality was legendary. A visit meant for "just ten minutes" that somehow turned into hours for me and Mitu (my wife), always ending with a dining table under the weight of *pakhala, badi,* and *maccha bhaja,* and *rabidi,* so aromatic it awakened Odia cravings. To eat at her table was to be seen, to be embraced, to be reminded that you belonged there. Even in her later years, when illness began to claim her strength, this generosity never waned—delicious *rabidi* will still come out of her kitchen, standing at the stove for about 8 hours, carefully cooked from regular milk to viscous rosy liquid. She might look weary, but if you walked through her door, she would spring to life, refusing to let sickness eclipse the warmth she carried. It was her way of defying decline, a declaration that joy and care would remain resilient like her.

Her final years were a test of endurance, and Lata Nani met them with poise. As doctors booked her calendar with endless appointments including managing the dangerous

COVID, she could find time to give us more than we could do, to return her warmth. That ability to laugh at pain was her form of resistance, a strength unmatched by medicine. By her side, through every storm stood our dear "Sashi bhaina" , her husband, whose presence was the silent proof of their shared resilience. Their story was not one of grand gestures, but of daily devotion, the quiet ride to the hospital, the shared meal, the clasped hands that whispered, "we can beat it together Lata." They weathered the unstageable play of illness, and when the final curtain fell, she parted with dignity, tethered to her love until the very end.

When we remember Lata Nani now, we know Lata Nani was never a "vine" her name might suggest. She was a big maple tree, firmly rooted in generosity, shading many lives, and living fully until the last. Her branches stretched across continents, making Odia culture visible through the lenses of *Champu, Chhanda,* and classical dramas. She was visible in her family room, ambidextrous in her kitchen, and unforgettable in her welcome. After more than fifty years in America, she remained unwaveringly Odia, taught us that culture lives not in monuments but in songs, laughter, food, and shared evenings of drama and melodious music. She is gone, yes—but her *Champu* and *Chhanda* still hum in the background, her hospitality still carries her smile, and her plays still echo with applause. She lived as a cultural icon until the last whistle drew the curtain. She was a maple tree whose shade endured in the memory of all who ever sat beneath it. Pranam to our immortal Lata Nani.

■

Ph.D., SCOR-P

My Personal Recollection of Lata Nani

Rosy Biswal

It is always an honor to remember and celebrate a very special lady — Lata Nani — the founder of Champu Chanda and a pillar of our community. For so many of us, she was not only the heart of this competition, but truly the heart of our Oriya community here in New Jersey and beyond. Through her kindness, her warmth, and her unwavering affection, she created a space where everyone felt welcome and valued.

She believed deeply in the power of music to connect people. To her, singing was never just about performance — it was about preserving our traditions, carrying forward our heritage, expressing ourselves, and sharing joy with others. She especially encouraged the children. She wanted every child to sing proudly, to embrace our culture, and to stand on stage with confidence.

I remember her encouraging our kids, especially my daughter Neha, when she was a little girl. Lata Nani told her, "Just sing from your heart, the rest will follow." She also gave Neha and Ellie $100 cash prizes for performing — a gesture that made the children feel so special and seen. That memory has stayed with me, and it is just one of the many examples of how she touched lives with her words, her generosity, and her presence.

What made her truly extraordinary was the way she carried her love and care into every corner of her life. She made the most delicious homemade desserts, and even when she was in a wheelchair, she insisted on preparing sweets herself. She never let her physical challenges stop her from giving to others. She also made it a point to call me every single week without fail — just to check in, just to share her warmth.

Even when she could barely walk, she thought of others first. She bought sarees for all of us, filling an entire suitcase with them, because she wanted to bring joy and beauty into our lives. These acts of kindness, big and small, showed the depth of her heart and the strength of her spirit.

Together with Saradendu Bhaina, she showed us that music was a celebration, not just a competition, and that togetherness was what truly mattered. Through her, we learned that tradition lives on when we nurture it with love.

Though she is no longer with us, her spirit remains present in every song sung on this stage, in every sweet we taste, in every saree we wear, and in every gathering of our community. Her legacy lives on through Champu Chanda and through the countless lives she touched with her kindness.

We love her, we miss her dearly, and we will always carry her spirit forward — in our music, in our traditions, and in the way we treat one another.

■

Lata Nani....a Multifaceted Personality

Litu Panda

It feels like yesterday when I got the phone call from Lata nani around 10 pm. "Can you please provide some home cooked food for bhaina? He doesn't like the food provided by the rehab. " Her voice was trembling, concerned yet strong. There was an inner urgency. Sashi bhaina was down with COVID and was recuperating in rehab. Lata nani was home sick with COVID.

If I remember correctly, this happened not long before she passed away. Till her last breath, she was always concerned for bhaina, worrying how he would cope with life without her.

Once Lata nani told me, "You know, there is a huge age gap between us. I always thought that I would take care of him during his old days. Now look who's doing what for whom. I could have managed without him, but he would find it very hard without me." Then she would get teary-eyed.

As I reflect on my time with her, I realize we knew Lata nani maybe for the last ten years of her life, yet I still have so many unforgettable memories of her. Those few years were nothing short of a beautiful book of emotions; her love and caring nature that will be etched in my life forever. Her warm demeanor, vibrancy, and enthusiasm for anything new always shone in a big gathering. She had a fine sense of fashion and was the soul of any crowd, and we used to welcome her presence as a gift of joy. I am fortunate, indeed, to have spent some time with her, before she breathed her last!

Another aspect of her life was her fearless nature. Lata nani was a courageous and a no-nonsense woman, fiercely opposing anything unjust and unfair. She would raise her voice and extend her hand for anyone entangled in a helpless situation.

Though death is an eternal fact of life, we miss you a lot Lata nani,and may you bless us to carry forward your legacy.

■

Mishra Aunty: Forever in Our Hearts

Anupama Tripathy

When I think of Mishra aunty, words seem inadequate to capture the extraordinary woman she was. She defied simple labels – she was simultaneously a mother figure, a spirited friend, a wise mentor, and so much more. To my daughters, she was a grandmother in every way that mattered, yet they called her "Mishra aunty" just as I did, because her vibrant, youthful spirit could never be contained by conventional titles. I was always in awe of her multifaceted presence in our lives.

I believe the universe was watching over me when it sent Mishra Uncle and Aunty to become my family away from family. As someone from Uttar Pradesh, raised as a military child across different parts of India, I found myself in unfamiliar territory when I married into an Odia family and immediately moved to the United States. With no family or friends nearby, and having never lived with my in-laws to learn their traditions, I knew little about Odisha beyond what I had read in school textbooks. The rich heritage and culture of this beautiful state remained a mystery to me.

I consider myself extraordinarily fortunate that we met Mishra aunty and uncle, who embraced us as family from the very beginning. They stood by us through every season of life – celebrations and sorrows, milestones and everyday moments. From my children's baby showers and births to their first birthdays, from housewarmings to Diwalis and New Year celebrations, no significant occasion felt complete without their presence.

Mishra aunty became the bridge that connected me to my adopted heritage. Through her, we joined the Odia Society of the Americas, where we met wonderful people and began to truly understand the depth and richness of Odia culture. Without her guidance and uncle's support, I would never have had the opportunity to learn about and experience the traditions that have now become such an important part of our family's identity. She opened not just her heart to us, but an entire world of cultural understanding.

What amazed us most was aunty's extraordinary persona – her petite, delicate frame housed a personality of incredible depth and dimension. She possessed that rare gift of connecting effortlessly with people of all ages, making everyone feel valued and understood. Her culinary skills were legendary. She could transform simple ingredients into feasts that would satisfy a houseful of guests in just a couple of hours, cooking with both skill and generous love. But her talents extended far beyond the kitchen. She was an accomplished actor, a graceful dancer, and above all, a passionate music enthusiast. She and uncle shared our love for classic Hindi songs, and I treasure the countless hours we spent listening to and singing melodies from old Bollywood films together.

One of her most significant contributions was her dedication to preserving and promoting Odia classical and folk music. Thanks to her efforts, these beautiful traditions continue to thrive today. I feel immense pride knowing that my own daughter learned and sings those songs because of aunty's influence – a living testament to her cultural legacy.

Among aunty's many admirable qualities, I was always moved by her authenticity. She spoke from her heart with refreshing honesty, showing a courage and directness that was both rare and inspiring. But what elevated her above all else was her unwavering passion for art and culture. She was a true ambassador – someone who didn't just appreciate these treasures but actively worked to share them with others and ensure their continuation.

People like Mishra aunty are born rarely, and the world is dimmer without her physical presence. Yet I find comfort knowing that while we cannot see her smile or hear her laughter anymore, her spirit lives on in countless ways – in the songs my daughter sings, in the traditions we continue to celebrate, in the warmth we show to others as she showed to us, and most importantly, in the love that forever binds our hearts to hers. She was, and always will be, a beautiful soul who touched our lives in ways that will echo through generations.

■

My journey with a legacy

Riti Mohanty

The place was Bridgewater, New Jersey. The date, a clear Saturday, August 9th, 2006.

That evening marked my debut as a singer in New Jersey, a performer still barely known by anyone. The occasion: a concert stage arranged for the legendary Tansen Singh.

Yet, the true source of my anxiety wasn't the stage itself, but the task ahead: a duet with a star singer from Odisha, and having the formidable Lata Apa as the emcee.

Her strong, commanding presence and the sheer weight of the moment gripped me. The prospect of performing alongside such talent, under her watchful eye, was overwhelming.

Looking back on that day now, I realize the immense pressure was instantly calmed by her nature.

I found her to be the shadow of a banyan tree—a sprawling, rooted strength that offered shade and refuge to the young sapling standing in its presence.

Our interaction began simply, with a polite monthly touch-base call. Yet, the connection quickly took root, and soon that monthly check-in became a customary weekly call. If one was missed, a fond complaint was anticipated, a gentle sign of the closeness we'd quickly drawn into.

My background as a singer secured me special attention and admiration, but over time, that initial interest blossomed into something far more profound. With every passing week, a boundless bond developed, evolving our relationship into one where the feeling of gratitude was constant, and deeply felt.

Lata Apa, though never formally trained, was legendary in the elderly circle for her singing skill. Tragically, my association with her coincided with the fading phase of her life, and I never witnessed her on a concert stage.

However, our shared passion for singing allowed me to truly cherish her artistic spirit. As a dramatist, she was brilliant, particularly in her roles as an actor and director. Her notable plays—*Patent Medicine, Kali-jai, Rebati, Nadha-Mundia Driver, and Ae Rango Rahele Hela*—are still top-of-mind and deeply revered.

For my part, I often contributed as a music composer and playback singer in many of these productions, allowing me to find a greater space in the cultural arena.

We grew even closer when she regularly visited our home to direct the social drama, *Facetime,* a play that brought us together as a family, especially since Sashi Bahina was acting in it as well.

The most striking memory echoes often: Three days before Lata Apa was admitted to the hospital, she called. Her voice held a specific urgency.

"Tell Chandra Sekhar to write a drama for me," she

pleaded. "Something that will let me live a little longer."

Her amazing love for drama was alive, even then. She was particularly interested in a historical plot: Sanjukta and Prithviraj, where she declared, "Sashi Bhaina will act too."

"Will he play the role of Sanjukta's father?" I asked, curiously.

Lata Apa immediately replied with characteristic boldness: "No. He will sit as a king in the Swayamvara Sabha (the bride-choosing assembly)."

I would try to evoke fun years later by referring to this memory—the idea of Bhaina participating as a king rather than a father—but internally, I always wondered at the depth of their love. How could they live without each other?

The dream, however, was blocked by reality. The COVID-19 lockdown came, and Lata Apa's wish to stage the play was never fulfilled.

She left us on an auspicious day, July 11th, 2021—the day of Ratha Yatra.

Days passed to years, and finally, Lata Apa's dream was realized on her first death anniversary.

The "Sanjukta and Prithviraj" play was staged with a beautiful, realistic plot at the ISKCON temple. Eva Apa played the role of Lata Apa, and Sashi Bahina presented as a king with other kings played by Uma Bahi, and Sarju Bhai , helping to make it a joyous, sometimes humorous drama with a cast of many others.

The very script of the play embodied the dedication it took. It was written on the road to Boston; Singha Babu was driving while I wrote down the dialogues from him. We even held online rehearsals after arriving at the hotel.

Ritu and Pradip were instrumental in staging the drama, supported by a devoted team: Lipi, Lal Bhai, Tapan, Anu, Bijoy, Rima, Ranjan, Anni, Sagarika, Manasi, Aarati, Nrusingha, Duma, Simon, Annu Tripathi and Singha Babu. I cherish the memory of every participant who helped fulfill a great dramatist's final, beautiful wish. Shanti Apa's memoir speech made a lasting impression.

Even during the depressing days when Parkinson held Lata apa in its clutch, Sashi Bhaina held fast to a single thought: "Lata is ten years younger than me. I have to live for her. Who will take care of her after me?"

Lata Apa, for her part, exhibited a warrior attitude. She was living proof that disability is a disease only of the mind. Her strong will to survive endured as if it were an undeclared, sacred promise: to stay together forever. *To live with you and to die with you.*

But the undeclared promise was broken. Lata Apa passed away.

Sashi Bhaina was left behind—a lonely bird in the nest, having lost a wing and knowing he can never truly fly again.

Today, Sashi Bhaina strives to uphold Lata Apa's legacy, channeling his grief into purpose by supporting CCO. It is his way of ensuring her spirited contribution to the world continues.

I do remember Lata Apa's stand to support Champu, Chhanda and Odissi. She used to sing these types of traditional songs and was very interested in preserving our age old traditional values. As a critic of ultra modern songs, she had the choice to bring back Odia musical heritage.

Her conviction was clear and challenging: If the Bengali community could be so proud of their Rabindra Sangeet, then why shouldn't Odias have the same pride in Odissi? This cultural parallel fueled her desire to bring our traditional music back into the spotlight.

Lata Apa was aware that she had found a key ally in me. She knew my music background: I was an All India Radio artist and held two *Visharads* in Odissi and Hindustani vocals. Before marriage, I had even worked in a Central School and ran a family-based music school.

It was this deep background—where passion met profession—that impelled me to come forward when Lata Apa looked to me for teaching Odissi.

It was her vision, coupled with my commitment, that began a special partnership. And, to this day, the journey continues.

The history of the CCO (Chhampu, Chhanda, Odissi) program began at the OSA Convention in Trenton, New Jersey, in 2009. It launched, for the very first time, with just ten students: seven young artists from New Jersey and three others from California, Michigan, and Maryland.

That initial cohort was made up of Neha, Gargi, Lipika, Abhinav, Shivani, Shreya, Ayesha, Erica, Anannya, and Debansya. The foundation for the program's success was laid by the dedicated team of Ritu Mohapatra, Pradip Tripathi, and Pradeep Mohapatra, all under the leadership of then-OSA President, Lalatendu Mohanty.

But the true heart of the event was Lata Apa. She not only presided as a judge, but more importantly, she served as my day-to-day mentor and was the fiercest advocate for this program, fighting for it tooth and nail.

My personal journey with CCO started by training all the children, whether onsite or remotely over the phone. On the day of the event, I was honored to share the stage with Devaki Bhai and accompany the harmonium with me alongside Surendra Ray on the tabla.

A video recording of that inaugural program remains my greatest inspiration. To this day, I use it every year to prepare the introductory video for the CCO program—a powerful and heartfelt tribute to Lata Apa, whose determination made it all possible.

Lata Apa's profound connection to the program was formalized years later. Though a proposal to rename the program was first given in 2015, it was finally adopted in 2019: the program officially became the Lata Misra Champu Chhanda Odissi (CCO).

Even today, her spirit of support is kept alive by Sashi Bhaina. He continues to personally sponsor cash rewards for all participants, ensuring that every child is recognized. The only exceptions are the top winners, who receive their prizes directly from the OSA.

In her last appearance on the CCO stage, Lata Apa publicly announced Ritu and myself as her successors. Since that day, the program has grown, with more and more chapters coming out to train children who are developing into soothing singers.

Lata Apa was a powerful, strong personality who

was absolutely unwavering in her mission. She knew the value of the CCO and always kept her "stick to the ground" to secure the prime stage and prime time for the children.

Alongside Sashi Bhaina, they were known as the most respected and loved elderly couple in the Odia community, having earned deep affection and respect through decades of association. When they chose to *throw their weight* to promote the CCO, the community did not just listen—they obliged. Their words ensured the program's success.

The CCO quickly became the flagship for Odia traditional songs and music. Its impact wasn't confined to the major OSA conventions; local chapters across the country came forward as partners in this vital endeavor to save our cultural heritage. Our New Jersey chapter, acting as a pioneer, remains committed to facilitating CCO programs in all prime events.

We soon faced a consistent logistical challenge: finding proficient harmonium and tabla players for rehearsals and performances in every location was becoming difficult. This inspired the idea to create music tracks, allowing learners and performers to sing in a karaoke style.

Initially, Lata Apa was reluctant about the idea, favoring live instruments. However, she quickly realized its necessity and not only agreed but personally arranged for the project's promoters.

The recording of these tracks was a collaborative effort born of generosity. Shanti Nani and Uma Bhai open-heartedly helped Lata Apa financially to meet the production expenses. Our first batch saw twelve songs selected for recording music tracks by Nazia, and to date, we've produced more than sixty tracks. Ritu serves as the vital custodian, compiling all music CDs for distribution, while Lal Bhai assists by selling them at OSA conventions, aiming to recover at least the production cost.

In the absence of Lata Apa, Sashi Bhaina has assured us her legacy will continue. Yet, her absence is an undeniable and heavy setback. We struggle to generate the same intense interest for CCO, to fill the void as a vocal figure in all occasions, and, most importantly, to replace the fierce spirit that fought so fiercely for the cause.

Lata Apa was a fighter till her last breath. I don't recall her ever showing desperation or complaining about her physical condition. I have simply never seen a person so passionately devoted to acting and singing.

Despite her disabilities, her longing for life was an amazing spirit. She often asked me, "How can I sing? What kind of practices can I possibly take up now?"

I remember the moment clearly—perhaps seven or eight days before she passed. I was playing a recording of a CCO program from the OSA convention held in Houston that year.

As the music filled the room, her eyes shone with a glorifying glaze. I felt the warmth of her gaze, expressing a silent, profound pride. It was as if she were the recipient of a lifetime achievement award, realizing the beautiful and lasting legacy she had created.

"Lata Apa, will you hear 'Jho Champu'?" I asked. ..."Jhogadi Matra He Shyamo.."

Her closed eyes and motionless body offered no response. Yet, having sung her favorite songs countless times before, I knew she was listening. Sashi Bhaina stood beside her bed, his gaze fixed on her face, desperately searching for any strain of life.

Suddenly, his muffled voice choked with bewildered happiness: "Look, look! Lata's eyes are blinking! She is listening to you."

Singha Babu, observing the slow rhythm of her breathing, asked Bhaina, "Should I stay tonight?"

Bhaina, his voice now imbued with a quiet certainty, replied, "No need. Lata will sleep peacefully."

The next morning, I received the call. That night had been her last.

The artist is gone, but the mandate remains: The show must go on.

And so, her legacy continues today, living on vibrantly through the CCO.

■

Plainsboro, New Jersey

Remembering Lata Nani

Yasaswini Mohapatra (Annie)

I still recall her voice saying, "Annie, if you're free tomorrow, could you come over?" I replied, yes, Lata Nani." She told me, "Tomorrow is Janmashtami. I've brought new clothes for all my deities from India. Will you please help by changing the old ones and dressing them in the new attire?" I followed her wishes as she observed closely, ensuring everything was just right. Her perfectionism was unmatched—whether caring for her deities, choosing her own clothes, or perfecting her style, she truly stood apart even during her difficult times. While life has taught me endless lessons, I also learnt that small rituals of hers helped me understand the importance of focusing on what matters most and being consistent in how you honor those values.

The more we crossed paths, the greater my admiration and respect for her grew. She embodied the idea of a complete woman—not only skillful in handling the routines of home but also attentive to matters far beyond. So many cherished moments come to mind from my visits with her. On one occasion, she asked me to pick up a L'Oreal night cream for her. When I gave her the cream and asked "how come your skin is always glowing".., she took time out to show me how to care for my skin, how to do makeup, and much more. Her enthusiasm and energy—despite any suffering she might have quietly borne—always took me by surprise. There was always something new to learn from her vitality and wisdom.

Grace and poise defined her. That enchanting smile and her warmth will forever remain vivid in the minds of all who knew her. I deeply cherish the virtuous, fulfilled life she lived. In moments of sadness, there's solace in knowing the people we love never truly leave us. It fills me with pride to have known such a remarkable soul and shared even a small part of life's journey with her. May her blessings always surround and comfort us.

It's difficult now to see Bhaina alone in the house, missing her constant companionship beside him. As she clearly told us, we make sure to celebrate Bhaina's birthday.

"Annie, you are like my daughter, please make sure, even if I am gone—make sure Bhaina's birthday is always celebrated."

Yes, Lata Nani, we kept your word, celebrating and remembering you as we did. The beautiful memories you've left behind are treasures we'll cherish forever.

■

New Jersey

ମୋ କଲମରୁ ନେଇ କିଛି ଅନୁଭବ ଓ ଅଭିମତ

ଚନ୍ଦ୍ରା ମିଶ୍ର

ଲତା ମିଶ୍ରଙ୍କ ବିଷୟରେ କିଛି ଲେଖିବା ପାଇଁ ମେସେଜ୍ ଟିଏ ପାଇଲି ଆମ ନ୍ୟୁୟର୍କ ର ପ୍ରିୟ ଲଲାଟେନ୍ଦୁ ମହାନ୍ତିଙ୍କ ଠାରୁ। ମୁଁ ଆଉ ଲତା ଏକା ବୟସର ହେବା ଯୋଗୁ ମୁଁ ଅନେକ ସମୟ ତାଙ୍କ ସାଙ୍ଗରେ ନ୍ୟୁୟର୍କ/ ନ୍ୟୁଜର୍ସି ଚାପ୍ଟ ର ରେ ହେଉଥିବା ବିଭିନ୍ନ କାର୍ଯ୍ୟରେ କଟାଇଥିଲି। ଗଣେଶ ପୂଜା, ସରସ୍ୱତୀ ପୂଜା, କୁମାର ପୂର୍ଣିମୀ ଆଉ ବାର୍ଷିକ ପିକନିକ୍ ରେ ଆମର ପ୍ରାୟ ଦେଖା ହୁଏ। ଏହା ବ୍ୟତୀତ ପିଲା ମାନଙ୍କର ଜନ୍ମ ଦିନ, ବାହାଘର ଏବଂ ସ୍କୁଲ ଗ୍ରାଜୁଏସନ୍ ପାର୍ଟିରେ ଆମର ଦେଖା ବି ହେଉଥଲା। ଓଡ଼ିଶାରୁ ସେତେବେଳେ ଆମେରିକାକୁ ବହୁତ କମ୍ ଓଡ଼ିଆ ଲୋକ ଆସୁଥିଲେ। ତେଣୁ ପ୍ରାୟ ସମସ୍ତେ ସମସ୍ତଙ୍କୁ ଓଡ଼ିଶାରୁ ଜାଣିଥିଲେ ବା ପରେ ମିଶି ତାଙ୍କୁ ଜାଣୁଥିଲେ। ସେଇ ପରି ପରିସ୍ଥିତିରେ ଆଗରୁ ନ ଜାଣିଲେ ବି ମୁଁ ଲତା ମିଶ୍ରକୁ ଜାଣି ଯାଇଥିଲି ସଭାରେ ଏକାଠି ହୋଇ। ଆମେ ଏକା ବୟସର ହୋଇ ଥିବାରୁ ବିଭିନ୍ନ ବିଷୟ ନେଇ ଗପ କରୁଥିଲୁ। ସେ ଅନୁଭବଗୁଡ଼ିକ ଏବେବି ଚଳଚିତ୍ର ପରି ମୋ ଆଖିରେ ନାଚି ଯାଏ। ଭିନ୍ନ ଥିଲା ସେ କଥା ସବୁ। ଲତାଙ୍କ ବିଷୟରେ ଅନୁଭବ ଗୁଡିକ ମୋ ପାଇଁ ଏକ ଉତ୍ସାହରେ ପରିପୂର୍ଣ୍ଣ ଯାତ୍ରା ଭଳି କହିଲେ ଅତ୍ୟୁକ୍ତି ହେବନି। ଏହା ଏମିତି ଯାତ୍ରା, ଯେଉଁଠି ମୁଁ ତାଙ୍କ ବିଷୟରେ ଅନେକ କଥା ଜାଣି ଥିଲେବି କେଉଁଠାରୁ ଆରମ୍ଭ କରି କେଉଁଠାରେ ଶେଷ କରିବି ନିଜେ ଜାଣି ପାରୁନି। ତାଙ୍କ ବ୍ୟକ୍ତିତ୍ୱକୁ ବଖାଣିଲା ବେଳେ ଶବ୍ଦ ଯୋଗାଡି ହୁଏନି ଯେହେତୁ ତାଙ୍କର ପ୍ରତିଭାର ଅବଦାନ ଆମ ପ୍ରବାସୀ ଓଡ଼ିଆଙ୍କ ପାଇଁ ଅନେକ।

ତାଙ୍କୁ ମୁଁ ଅନେକ ଯାଗାରେ ଭେଟିଛି। ପ୍ରବାସରେ ରହିଥିବା ଓଡ଼ିଆମାନେ ଆମେ ବର୍ଷରେ ଦୁଇ ତିନି ଦିନ ଓ.ସ.ଏ.(Odisha Society of America)

ସମ୍ମେଳନରେ ଗୋଟିଏ ଯାଗାରେ ଏକାଠି ହୋଇ ଖାଇବା,ଗଳ୍ପ କରିବା ଓ ମଂଚରେ ପିଲା ଓ ବଡ଼ ମାନଙ୍କର ନାଟକ, ଗୀତ, ନାଚ ଦେଖିବାର ସୁଯୋଗ ପାଇଥାଉ। ବର୍ଷକରେ ଥରେ ଜୁଲାଇ ମାସରେ ପ୍ରବାସରେ ଥିବା ଓଡ଼ିଆ ଲୋକ ମାନଙ୍କୁ କିପରି ଏକାଠି କରି ଆମ ସଂସ୍କୃତି, କଳା (ଗୀତ, ନାଚ, ଚିତ୍ରକଳା) ଓ ଭାଷାକୁ ବଂଚାଇ ରଖି ପାରିବୁ ସେ ବିଷୟରେ ଆଲୋଚନା କରୁ। ବିଭିନ୍ନ ସେମିନାର ଆଉ ସଭା ହୁଏ ଯେଉଁଠି ଅନେକ ବିଷୟ ଚର୍ଚ୍ଚା ହୁଏ। ଓଡ଼ିଶାରୁ ବିଶିଷ୍ଟ କଳାକାର ଓ ରାଜନେତାମାନେ ଏହି ସଭାକୁ ଆମନ୍ତ୍ରିତ ହୋଇ ଆସନ୍ତି। ଓଡ଼ିଶୀ ସଙ୍ଗୀତ ଭାରତର ଶାସ୍ତ୍ରୀୟ ସଙ୍ଗୀତର ଗୋଟିଏ ବିଶେଷ ଶୈଳୀ, ଯାହାର ମୂଳ ଉତ୍ସ ଓଡ଼ିଶାର ଗୀତ ଚମ୍ପୁ, ଛାନ୍ଦ। ଚମ୍ପୁ ଓଡ଼ିଆ କାବ୍ୟରେ ଶୈଳୀ ଓ ସାରଗର୍ଭୀତ ପ୍ରକାର। ଛାନ୍ଦ ହେଉଛି ସଙ୍ଗୀତିକ ଆତ୍ମା, ଯାହା ଗୀତ ଓ କବିତାକୁ ଲୟମୟ କରେ।

ଲତା ମିଶ୍ର ଚମ୍ପୁ, ଛାନ୍ଦ ଗୀତ ଆମର ଓଷା ସମ୍ମିଳନରେ ସବୁବେଳେ ଗାଉଥିଲେ। ଗତ କିଛି ବର୍ଷ ଧରି ଓଷା ସମ୍ମେଳନରେ ଓଡ଼ିଶୀ, ଚମ୍ପୁ ଓ ଛାନ୍ଦ ସଙ୍ଗୀତ ପ୍ରତିଯୋଗିତା- ଜୁନିଅର ଓ ସିନିଅର- ଦୁଇଟି ବୟସ ଶ୍ରେଣୀ ପାଇଁ ଆୟୋଜିତ ହେଉଛି।

ଏହି କାର୍ଯ୍ୟକ୍ରମର ପ୍ରବର୍ତ୍ତକା ଥିଲେ ଲତା ମିଶ୍ର। ଆଜିକାଲି ଅଧିକାଂଶ ଗାୟକ ହିନ୍ଦୀ ଚଳଚ୍ଚିତ୍ର ସଙ୍ଗୀତକୁ ପସନ୍ଦ କରନ୍ତି, ତଥାପି ଲତା ପ୍ରବାସରେ ହେଉଥିବା ପ୍ରତି କାର୍ଯ୍ୟକ୍ରମରେ ପାରମ୍ପରିକ ଚମ୍ପୁ ଓ ଛାନ୍ଦକୁ ଅବିରତ ଗାଇବା ପାଇଁ ନିର୍ଣ୍ଣୟ ନେଇଥିଲେ। ସେ ଆମ ପ୍ରବେଶ ରେ ହେଉଥିବା ସମାରୋହରେ ଓଡ଼ିଶୀ ଚମ୍ପୁ, ଛାନ୍ଦ ଗାଉଥିଲେ- ସେତେବେଳେ ଏ ପ୍ରକାର ଗୀତ ଗାଇବା ପାଇଁ କୌଣସି ପ୍ରକାର ସାଧନ ବାଜନା ନ ଥିଲା। ପିଲାଦିନେ ସିଏ କୌଣସି ପ୍ରକାର ଗୀତ ବି ଶିଖି ନ ଥିଲେ। କେବଳ ତାଙ୍କ ବାପା ଆଉ କକେଇଙ୍କଠାରୁ ଗୀତ ଶୁଣି ଗୀତ ଗାଉଥିଲେ। ତାଙ୍କର ସ୍ୱର ଅତି ସୁନ୍ଦର ଥିଲା। ତାହା ମା ସରସ୍ୱତୀଙ୍କର କୃପା ବୋଲି ସିଏ କୁହନ୍ତି ଆମ ସମସ୍ତଙ୍କୁ।

ଆଜିକାଲି ଅଧିକାଂଶ ପିଲାମାନେ ହିନ୍ଦୀ ଚଳଚ୍ଚିତ୍ର ସଙ୍ଗୀତକୁ ପସନ୍ଦ କରନ୍ତି। କିନ୍ତୁ ତାହା ସତ୍ତ୍ୱେ ଲତା ପାରମ୍ପରିକ ଚମ୍ପୁ ଓ ଛାନ୍ଦକୁ ଚାଲୁ ରଖିବା ଓ ତାହାକୁ ପ୍ରଚାର କରିବାରେ ଦୃଢ଼ ନିଷ୍ପତ୍ତି ନେଇଥିଲେ। ଏହା ନିଶ୍ଚୟ ତାଙ୍କର ଦୃଢ଼ ମନର ଉଦାହରଣ ଓ ପ୍ରଶଂସନୀୟ।

ଅନେକ ଲୋକ ଭାବିଥିଲେ ଯେ ସେମାନଙ୍କ ପିଲାମାନେ ସମ୍ଭବତଃ ଓଡ଼ିଆ ପାରମ୍ପରିକ ସଙ୍ଗୀତ ଶିଖିବାକୁ ଇଚ୍ଛା କରିବେ ନାହିଁ, କିମ୍ବା ସେଥିପାଇଁ ସମୟ ଦେଇ ପାରିବେ ନାହିଁ। କିନ୍ତୁ ଲତା, ପିଲାମାନଙ୍କୁ ଆଉ ତାଙ୍କ ଅଭିଭାବକମାନଙ୍କୁ ଏହି ସଙ୍ଗୀତ ଶିଖିବାର ମହତ୍ତ୍ୱ ବିଷୟରେ ବୁଝେଇବାରେ ସଫଳ ହୋଇଥିଲେ। ଏବେ

ଆମେରିକାରେ ବିଭିନ୍ନ ଯାଗାରେ ଅନେକ ପିଲାମାନେ ଏହି ପାରମ୍ପରିକ ସଙ୍ଗୀତ ଶିଖିବା ପାଇଁ ଆଗ୍ରହୀ ହୋଇ ପାରିଛନ୍ତି। ସେ ସମୟ ଓ ଶ୍ରମ ଦୁଇଟି ଅଭିଭାବକ ଓ ପିଲାମାନଙ୍କ ପାଇଁ ଦେଇଥିଲେ, ଯାହାଦ୍ୱାରା ପିଲାମାନେ ଏହି ସଙ୍ଗୀତକୁ ଶିଖିବାରେ ଓ ଭଲପାଇବାରେ ସଫଳ ହୋଇଛନ୍ତି।

ଆଜିକାଲି ଆମେରିକାରେ ଅନେକ ଯୁବ ଅଭିଭାବକ ଓ ପିଲାମାନେ ଏହି ସଙ୍ଗୀତକୁ ଶିଖୁଛନ୍ତି ଏବଂ ବିଭିନ୍ନ ମଞ୍ଚରେ ସୁନ୍ଦର ଗାୟନରେ ଦର୍ଶକ ମାନଙ୍କୁ ଆଶ୍ଚର୍ଯ୍ୟ କରୁଛନ୍ତି । ଏଇ ଉଦାହରଣ ଦେଖି ମତେ ମୋର ପ୍ରିୟ ବ୍ୟକ୍ତି, ପୂର୍ବତନ ପ୍ରଥମ ଲେଡି ଏଲେନର୍ ରୁଜଭେଲ୍ଟ ଙ୍କର ଏକ ଉକ୍ତି ସ୍ମରଣ କରାଏ-

"ଆମେ ଯାହା କରିପାରିବୁନି ବୋଲି ଭାବୁଥାଉ, ସେଇ କାମକୁ କରିବାକୁ ଆମକୁ ଚେଷ୍ଟା କରିବା ଦରକାର। "

ଲତା ମିଶ୍ର ସେହି କଥାକୁ ପ୍ରମାଣ କରିଛନ୍ତି। ଆମେ ଯେତେବେଳେ ସନ୍ଦେହ କରୁଥିଲୁ, କିପରି ଆମ ପିଲାମାନେ ଚମ୍ପୁ, ଛାନ୍ଦ ଶିଖିବେ ଆଉ ମଞ୍ଚରେ ପରିବେଷଣ କରିବେ, ସେ ତାହା କରି ଆମ ସମସ୍ତଙ୍କୁ ଚକିତ କରିଛନ୍ତି। ଓଷା ସମ୍ମେଳନରେ କିମ୍ୱା ଅନ୍ୟାନ୍ୟ ସ୍ଥାନରେ ଯୁବ ଓଡ଼ିଆ ପିଲାମାନେ ମଞ୍ଚରେ ଚମ୍ପୁ ଓ ଛାନ୍ଦ ଗାଉଥିବା ଦେଖିବା, ଆମ ପାଇଁ ଏକ ଅତ୍ୟନ୍ତ ସୁଖଦ ଅନୁଭବ।

ଚମ୍ପୁ, ଛାନ୍ଦ ବ୍ୟତୀତ ଲତା ଓଡ଼ିଆ ନାଟକ ଅଭିନୟ କରିବାରେ ନିପୁଣ ଥିଲେ ଆଉ ସମସ୍ତଙ୍କୁ ମଞ୍ଚରେ ଅଭିନୟ କରିବାକୁ ଉତ୍ସାହିତ କରୁଥିଲେ। ପେଟେଣ୍ଟ ମେଡ଼ିସିନ୍ ନାଟକରେ ସାଆନ୍ତାଣିଙ୍କ ଅଭିନୟରୁ ଦର୍ଶକ ମାନେ ଦେଖିଲେ ଜାଣି ପାରିବେ ସେ କିପରି ଏକ ଉଚ୍ଚ କୋଟିର ଅଭିନେତ୍ରୀ ଥିଲେ। ଯଦିଓ ସେ କୌଣସି ସ୍କୁଲ୍‌ରେ ନାଟକ କିମ୍ୱା ସଙ୍ଗୀତ ଶିଖିନଥିଲେ, ତଥାପି ମଞ୍ଚରେ ଯେତେବେଳେ ସେ ଥାଆନ୍ତି, ସେ ଆତ୍ମବିଶ୍ୱାସୀ ଶିଳ୍ପୀ ଭାବରେ ଅଭିନୟ କରୁଥିଲେ । ସେ ଅତ୍ୟନ୍ତ କଳ୍ପନାଶୀଳ ମଣିଷ ଥିଲେ- ଯାହା ମଞ୍ଚଶିଳ୍ପୀଙ୍କ ପାଇଁ ସର୍ବଶ୍ରେଷ୍ଠ ଗୁଣମାନଙ୍କ ମଧ୍ୟରୁ ଗୋଟିଏ।

ଲତା ସବୁବେଳେ ଇଚ୍ଛା କରୁଥିଲେ, କିପରି ଆହୁରି ଭଲ ଅଭିନୟ ମଞ୍ଚରେ କରିପାରିବେ। ନିଜର ଅଭିନୟ ହେଉ ବା ଗୀତ ଗାଇବା ହେଉ ତାକୁ ସିଏ ସୁଧାରିବାକୁ ସବୁବେଳେ ଚେଷ୍ଟା କରୁଥିଲେ। ଆମେ ସମସ୍ତେ, ତାଙ୍କର ଏହି ପ୍ରଗତିର ସାକ୍ଷୀ ଆଉ ସେ ସବୁ ନିଜ ଆଖିରେ ଦେଖିଛୁ। ଉତ୍କୃଷ୍ଟ ଅଭିନୟ ସେତେବେଳେ ଘଟେ, ଯେତେବେଳେ ଭିତରୁ ଓ ବାହାରୁ- ଦୁହିଁଙ୍କୁ ସମୟକୁଳେ ପ୍ରଦର୍ଶନ କରାଯାଏ।

ଲତା, ସେହି କଳାକୁ ଭଲଭାବେ ଆତ୍ମସାତ କରିଥିଲେ।

କଳା ପ୍ରତି ତାଙ୍କର ଅବଦାନ ପାଇଁ ୨୦୦୪ ମସିହାରେ ଡାଲାସ୍

ସମ୍ମେଳନରେ, ସେ ଓଷା ପକ୍ଷରୁ କଳାଶ୍ରୀ ସମ୍ମାନ ପାଇଥିଲେ। ଆମ ଓଷା ନ୍ୟୁଜର୍ସି, ନ୍ୟୁଅର୍କର ମଞ୍ଚରେ ହେଉଥିବା ସମସ୍ତ କାମରେ ସେ ଯୁବ ପିଢିଙ୍କୁ ନିର୍ଦ୍ଦେଶନା ଦେଇ ଉତ୍ସାହିତ କରୁଥିଲେ। ପରେ ସିଏ ଅସୁସ୍ଥ ଥିବା ସତ୍ତ୍ୱେ ଚକଚଏୟାର ଉପରେ ବସି ଯୁବକ, ଯୁବତୀ ଓ ପିଲା ମାନଙ୍କର ପଥପ୍ରଦର୍ଶକ ହୋଇଥିଲେ ମଞ୍ଚରେ। ତାଙ୍କ ଭଳି ନିଷ୍ଠାବାନ ଓ ପରିଶ୍ରମୀ ବ୍ୟକ୍ତିମାନଙ୍କ କାରଣରୁ, ଆମେ ଆମର ସଙ୍ଗୀତ ଓ ନାଟକ ଉପଭୋଗ କରିପାରୁଥିଲୁ ଆଉ ଏହା, ଆମର ନଷ୍ଟାଲଜିଆ (ସ୍ମୃତିବିଳାସ) କୁ ସନ୍ତୁଷ୍ଟ କରିଥିଲା- ଓଡ଼ିଶାର 'ପୁରୁଣା ସଙ୍ଗୀତ ଶୁଣିବା ଓ ପୁରୁଣା ନାଟକ ଦେଖିବା'।

ବ୍ୟକ୍ତିଗତ ଦୃଷ୍ଟିରୁ, ଯାହା ମତେ / ଆମ ସମସ୍ତଙ୍କୁ ଆଶ୍ଚର୍ଯ୍ୟ କରେ, ସେହେଲା — ପରିସ୍ଥିତିକୁ ଗ୍ରହଣ କରିବାରେ ଲତାଙ୍କର ଅଦ୍ଭୁତ ଦୃଷ୍ଟିଭଙ୍ଗୀ। ହସ୍ପିଟାଲରେ ନର୍ସ ଭାବରେ କାମ କଲା ବେଳେ ମୁଁ ଅନେକ ରୋଗୀ ଯେଉଁମାନେ ଏଇ ପାର୍କିନ୍ସନ୍ ରୋଗରେ ପୀଡିତ ହୋଇ ଥାଆନ୍ତି ସେମାନଙ୍କର ଶାରୀରିକ ଆଉ ମାନସିକ ଅବସ୍ଥା ଭଲ ନ ଥାଏ। ଲତା ପାର୍କିନସନ୍ ରୋଗ ସହିତ ଅନେକ ବର୍ଷ ଯୁଦ୍ଧ କରିଛନ୍ତି, ଯାହା ବହୁତ ଚାଲେଞ୍ଜିଂ ଥିଲା। ତଥାପି, ସେ କୌଣସି କାର୍ଯ୍ୟକ୍ରମକୁ ଯିବା ବନ୍ଦ କରିନଥିଲେ ଶେଷ ପର୍ଯ୍ୟନ୍ତ। ଥରେ ମୁଁ ତାଙ୍କୁ ସାଙ୍ଗଭାବେ ପଚାରିଲି- "ହ୍ୱିଲଚେୟାରରେ ଥିବାବେଳେ, କାମ କରିବା କେତେ କଷ୍ଟକର?"

ସେ ହସି ଦେଇ କହିଥିଲେ- "ଆମେ ଶବ୍ଦକୋଷକୁ ବଦଳାଇବା ଉଚିତ୍ 'ମୁଁ କରିପାରିବି', 'ମୁଁ କରିପାରିବିନି' ନୁହେଁ। ତାହାହେଲେ, ଆମେ ପ୍ରକୃତରେ ସଫଳ ମଣିଷ ବୋଲି କହି ପାରିବା।

ସେ ନ୍ୟୁୟର୍କ–ନ୍ୟୁଜର୍ସି ସମୁଦାୟର ଯୁବ ପିଢ଼ି ସହ ଏକ ସମର୍ଥନର ଜାଲ ଗଢ଼ିଥିଲେ। ସମସ୍ତେ, ତାଙ୍କୁ ଦେଖି ପ୍ରେରିତ ହେଉଥିଲେ ଓ ତାଙ୍କ ଦୃଷ୍ଟିକୋଣକୁ ସାର୍ଥକ କରିବାକୁ ଚେଷ୍ଟା କରି ଆସିଛନ୍ତି।

ଉତ୍ତର ଆମେରିକାରେ ଓଡ଼ିଆ ନାଟକ ଓ ସଙ୍ଗୀତ ଚମ୍ପୁ, ଛାନ୍ଦକୁ ବଞ୍ଚାଇ ରଖିବା ପାଇଁ ତାଙ୍କର ଅବଦାନ ଅନେକ। ସେଥିପାଇଁ ଲତା ସବୁଦିନ ପାଇଁ ସ୍ମରଣୀୟ ହୋଇ ରହିବେ।

ଲତା ମିଶ୍ରଙ୍କର କୃତି ଲେଖିଲା ବେଳେ ତାଙ୍କ ସହିତ ମୋ ନିଜ ଅନୁଭବ କଥାଟି ନକହିଲେ ତାଙ୍କୁ ନେଇ ଦୀର୍ଘ ଲେଖାଟି ହୁଏତ ଅସାର ଲାଗିପାରେ । ବନ୍ଧୁତା ମୋ' ପାଇଁ ଇନ୍ଦ୍ରଧନୁ ସମ। କେତେ କେତେ ଅନୁଭବର ରଙ୍ଗରେ ବନ୍ଧୁତା ମୋ' ସକାଶେ ସୁଦୃଶ୍ୟ ଏବଂ ଈଶ୍ୱରୀୟତାର ପରିପ୍ରକାଶ। ୧୯୯୭ ମସିହାରେ ମୋ ଝିଅ ସୀମାର ବାହାଘର ଅତି ଅଳ୍ପ ସମୟ ଭିତରେ ଠିକ୍ ହୋଇଥିଲା। ଆଜି କାଲି ପରି ସେ

ସମୟରେ ଆମେରିକାରେ ବିବାହ ପାଇଁ ସବୁ ସରଞ୍ଜାମ ସୁବିଧାରେ ମିଳୁ ନ ଥିଲା। ଆମ ଘରୁ କେହି ଆସି ପାରି ନଥିଲେ ବାହାଘର ପାଇଁ। ସେ ସମୟରେ ଅନେକ ପ୍ରଥା ଲତା ମତେ ଟେଲିଫୋନ୍‌ରେ କହି ମୋ ମନରେ ସାହସ ଦେଇ ଥିଲେ। ଆମ ଓଡ଼ିଆ ପରମ୍ପରା ଭାବରେ ବାହାଘର ସମୟରେ ହୁଳହୁଳି ଆଉ ଶଙ୍ଖ ବଜାଇବାକୁ ଶୁଭ ବୋଲି କହିଥିଲେ। ଆମେ କେହି ଶଙ୍ଖ ଫୁଙ୍କିବା ପାରିବା ଜାଣି ନ ଥିବା ଜାଣି ସିଏ ନିଜେ ଶଙ୍ଖଫୁଙ୍କି ହୁଳ ହୁଳି ଦେଇ ଶୁଭ କାମଟିରେ ଆମକୁ ସାହାଯ୍ୟ କରିଥିଲେ। ମୋର ସମବୟସୀ ହେଲେବି ସିଏ ଆମେରିକାରେ ଅନେକ ଯଶ, ସମ୍ମାନ ସାଉଁଟି ଥିଲେ। ବେଳେ ବେଳେ ମୁଁ ଭାବେ ସେତିକି ସୁନାମ ଅର୍ଜି ନିଜର ନାଁ ଅର୍ଜିବାକୁ ଜଣଙ୍କୁ କେତେ ପରିଶ୍ରମ କରିବାକୁ ହେବ ? ପ୍ରତିଭା ଓ ପରିଚୟ ଈଶ୍ୱରଙ୍କ ଆଶୀର୍ବାଦ ଆଉ ସେହି ଦୃଷ୍ଟିକୋଣରୁ ସେ ଆଶୀର୍ବାଦିତ। ସେ ମଞ୍ଚରେ ଗୀତ ଗାଇବା ହେଉକି ନାଟକ ରେ ମୁଖ୍ୟ ଅଭିନେତ୍ରୀ ଭାବେ ଅଭିନୟ କରିବା ହେଉ ମୁଁ ଯେତିକି ଆଚମ୍ବିତ ହୁଏ ସେତିକି ବିସ୍ମିତ ହୁଏ ତାଙ୍କ କାମ କରିବାର ଶକ୍ତି ଦେଖି। ଘରକରଣା ସହ ଅଫିସ ସମ୍ଭାଳି ଓଡ଼ିଆ ସାନ ପିଲା ମାନଙ୍କୁ ଓଡ଼ିଆ ଚମ୍ପୁ , ଛାନ୍ଦ ଶିଖାଇବାର ସକ୍ରିୟତାରେ ସେ ନିପୁଣ ଥିଲେ। ମଞ୍ଚରେ ପିଲାଙ୍କ ସହ ଲତାଙ୍କର ଫଟୋ ଦେଖିଲେ ସୁକୁମାରତା ଓ ସ୍ନିଗ୍ଧତାର ଏକ କୋମଳ ଅନୁଭବ ମୋତେ ଧୀରେ ଛୁଇଁଦିଏ। ଗଛକୁ ସିଏ ବହୁତ ଭଲ ପାଉଥିଲେ। ତାଙ୍କ ଦେବା ମଲ୍ଲୀ ଗଛ ଏବେବି ଅନେକ ଲୋକଙ୍କର ଘରେ ତୋଫା ମଲ୍ଲୀ ଫୁଲ ଫୁଟାଇ ଘରକୁ ଶୋଭିତ ଆଉ ମହକିତ କରୁଛି ବୋଲି ମୁଁ ଶୁଣିବାକୁ ପାଉଛି। ତାଙ୍କ ସାହାଯ୍ୟ ଆଉ ବନ୍ଧୁତା ପାଇଁ ମୁଁ ନିହାତି ଭାବରେ କୃତଜ୍ଞ ରହିବି ସବୁ ଦିନ ପାଇଁ। ମୋ ସାନ ପୁଅ ବର୍ଷକର ହେଲାବେଳେ ପରେ ଲତା ତା ସାଙ୍ଗେ କଥା କହିବାକୁ ଚାହୁଁ ଥିବାର ଫୋଟୋଟିଏ ରଖୁଛି ଆମର ସ୍ମୃତି ଭାବେ। ସେତେବେଳେ ଆଜି କାଲି ପରି ଫୋଟୋ ଉଠାଇବା ଯୁଗ ନ ଥିଲା।

ଏବେ ବି କହିପାରେ ତାଙ୍କ ଭଳି ଗୁଣବତୀ, ସୁନ୍ଦରୀ ଏବଂ ପରିଶ୍ରମୀ ଝିଅ ବିରଳ ଆମ ଓଡ଼ିଆ ସମାଜରେ। ବିଧିରବିଧାନ ଥିଲା ଅଲଗା ନହେଲେ ଆଜି ସେ ଆମ ନ୍ୟୁୟର୍କ ଅଧ୍ୟାୟର ପିଲା ମାନଙ୍କୁ ଝଲସାଇ ଦେଇ ଥାଆନ୍ତେ ଚମ୍ପୁ, ଛାନ୍ଦ ଗୀତ ଦ୍ୱାରା ମଞ୍ଚରେ ସାରା ଆମେରିକାରେ। ମୋ ଲେଖାଟି ପଢି ପାଠକ ମାନେ ଲତା ମିଶ୍ରଙ୍କ ପ୍ରତିଭା, ଅବଦାନ ବିଷୟରେ କିଛି ଜାଣିଲେ ମୋର ଶ୍ରମ ସାର୍ଥକ ହେବ। ଶେଷରେ କହିବି- ତାଙ୍କ ବିଷୟରେ ଲେଖିବାର ସୁଯୋଗ ପାଇ ମୁଁ ଗର୍ବିତ ଅନୁଭବ କରୁଛି।

■

ଫିଲ୍‌ଡେଲ୍‌ଫିଆ

ସୁନା ଚିହ୍ନେ ବଣିଆ

ରିତୁ ମିଶ୍ର

ବନଲତା ଓରଫ୍ ଲତା ନାନୀ ! ପିଲାଦିନରୁ ଶୁଣିଆସିଥିଲି ଯେ ନାମ ସହିତ ବ୍ୟକ୍ତିତ୍ୱର ଏକ ଅଦୃଶ୍ୟ ସମ୍ବନ୍ଧ ରହିଥାଏ, ସେ ସମ୍ବନ୍ଧ ସମଧର୍ମୀ ଅଥବା ବିରୋଧାତ୍ମକ ହୋଇପାରେ; ଲତା ନାନୀଙ୍କ କ୍ଷେତ୍ରରେ ଏହି ବିଶେଷ କଥନ ସତ୍ୟ ପ୍ରମାଣିତ ହୋଇଥିଲା । ଯେପରି ଲତାଟିଏ ଆଶ୍ରା ଦେଇଥିବା ବୃକ୍ଷର ସୌନ୍ଦର୍ଯ୍ୟ ବଢ଼ାଏ, ସେହିପରି ମୋ ଲତା ନାନୀ ତାଙ୍କ ଦାମ୍ପତ୍ୟ ଜୀବନର ସୌନ୍ଦର୍ଯ୍ୟର ଉତ୍ସ ଥିଲେ । କିନ୍ତୁ ବଣ ଲତାର ଅନ୍ୟ ଏକ ଗୁଣ ଯାହାକି ଆଶ୍ରିତ ବୃକ୍ଷ ଉପରେ ନିର୍ଭରଶୀଳ ରହିବା, ଏହି ଗୁଣର ସମ୍ପୂର୍ଣ୍ଣ ବିପରୀତ ଥିଲା ଆମ ନାନୀଙ୍କ ବ୍ୟକ୍ତିତ୍ୱ । ତାଙ୍କର ନିଜସ୍ୱ ଚିନ୍ତାଧାରା, ସ୍ୱାଧୀନ ମତାମତ, ଏବଂ ନେତୃତ୍ୱ ନେବାର କ୍ଷମତା ତାଙ୍କ ନାମର ବିରୋଧାତ୍ମକ ସମ୍ବନ୍ଧକୁ ବୁଝାଉଥିଲା ।

ଲତା ନାନୀଙ୍କ ସହିତ ମୋର ପରିଚୟ ହୁଏ ୨୦୦୩ ମସିହା OSA conventionର ପ୍ରସ୍ତୁତି ପର୍ଯ୍ୟାୟରେ । ମୋର ବଡ଼ ନାନୀ ସମ ଇଭା ମହାନ୍ତି ମତେ Conventionର ପ୍ରାରମ୍ଭିକ ସାମୂହିକ ସଙ୍ଗୀତର କାର୍ଯ୍ୟକ୍ରମରେ ଯୋଗଦାନ ଦେବା ପାଇଁ କହିଲେ । ଲତା ନାନୀ ସେହି କାର୍ଯ୍ୟକ୍ରମର ତତ୍ତ୍ୱାବଧାନରେ ଥିଲେ । ସେହି ସମୟରୁ ଆମ ସମ୍ବନ୍ଧର ଡୋର କଷା ହୋଇଗଲା । ପ୍ରଥମେ ସେ ସମ୍ବନ୍ଧ ଦୁଇ ସଂଗୀତପ୍ରେମୀଙ୍କର ଭାବ ଆଦାନପ୍ରଦାନରୁ ଆରମ୍ଭ ହୋଇ କେତେବେଳେ ଯେ ଏକ ନିବିଡ ଆତ୍ମୀୟତାର ସମ୍ପର୍କରେ ପରିବର୍ତ୍ତିତ ହୋଇଗଲା, ତାହା ଏବେ ଭାବିଲେ ଆଶ୍ଚର୍ଯ୍ୟ ଲାଗେ ।

ଏହି ସମ୍ପର୍କର ଧାରାରେ ଆମର କେତେ ସମୟ ବିତିଯାଇଛି ସାହିତ୍ୟ ଚର୍ଚ୍ଚାରେ, ନାଟକ ଖୋଜା ଆଉ ଲେଖା, ଅଭିନେତା ଅଭିନେତ୍ରୀ ବଛାବଛିରେ, ପୁଣି ଚମ୍ପୁ, ଛାନ୍ଦ ଆଉ ଓଡ଼ିଶୀ (CCO) କାର୍ଯ୍ୟକ୍ରମର ସ୍ଥାପନ ଏବଂ ଅନୁରକ୍ଷଣରେ । ବହୁତ ସମୟରେ ମୁଁ ଅଭିଭୂତ ହୁଏ ଲତା ନାନୀଙ୍କର ବ୍ୟକ୍ତିତ୍ୱର ଭିନ୍ନ ଭିନ୍ନ ଦିଗ ର ପରିଚୟ ପାଇ ।

ଥରେ ରାତି ନଅଟା ଖଣ୍ଡେ ହେବ, ଫୋନ ଆସିଲା। ଫୋନ ଉଠାଉ ଉଠାଉ, ସେପଟୁ ଶୁଭିଲା ନାନୀଙ୍କ ବିରକ୍ତିରେ ଭରାସ୍ୱର 'ଆଚ୍ଛା କହିଲ, ଗାଈ ବାସୁଦେବଙ୍କର, ଷଣ୍ଢ ମହାଦେବଙ୍କର, ବଳଦ ବାପୁଡ଼ା କାହାର ନୁହେଁ ?' ଏହି ଢଗଟି ମୁଁ କାନ ଉଠିବା ଦିନରୁ ଶୁଣି ନଥିଲି। ମୁଁ କହିଲି 'ନାନୀ କ'ଣ କହୁଛନ୍ତି ମୁଁ ବୁଝିପାରୁନି?' ସ୍ୱରରେ ଅପର୍ଯ୍ୟାପ୍ତ ତିକ୍ତତା ଭରି କହିଲେ "OSA ଆ'ଙ୍କର, Convention ତା'ଙ୍କର, ହେଲେ CCO କାହାର ନୁହେଁ? କାହାର ଚିନ୍ତା ନାହିଁ CCO ପାଇଁ?" ମୋ ଭିତରେ ଏକ ମିଶ୍ର ଆବେଗର ଅନୁଭୂତି ହେଲା, ଓଡ଼ିଆ ଭାଷାରେ ନାନୀଙ୍କର ପ୍ରବୀଣତା ଏବଂ ଓଡ଼ିଶାର ସଂଗୀତ ପାଇଁ ଆନ୍ତରିକ ଭଲ ପାଇବାକୁ ଅନୁଭବ କରି! ଯେଉଁ ଥିରେ ବି ସେ ହାତ ଦେଉଥିଲେ, ସେଥିରେ ତାଙ୍କର ଶତ ପ୍ରତିଶତ ନିଷ୍ଠା ଏବଂ ପୂର୍ଣ୍ଣତା ପ୍ରଦାନ କରିବାର ଦୃଢ ସଂକଳ୍ପ ରହୁଥିଲା।

ମୋ ଲତା ନାନୀଙ୍କର ସବୁଠୁ ବଡ ଦକ୍ଷତା ଥିଲା କାହା ଭିତରର ଲୁକ୍କାୟିତ ଗୁଣକୁ ଚିହ୍ନିବା, ଆଉ ସେଇ ଗୁଣକୁ ଲୋକଲୋଚନକୁ ଆଣିବା।

ଗୁଣ ଚିହ୍ନେ ଗୁଣିଆ
ସୁନା ଚିହ୍ନେ ବଣିଆ

'ବୁଝିଲ, ମୁଁ ପାଇଗଲି ଆମ ଡ୍ରାମାର heroinକୁ। କାଲି ଆମ ଘରକୁ ଅମୁକ ଝିଅଟି ଆସିଥିଲା। ତା'ର କଥା କହିବା ଢଙ୍ଗରୁ ପୂରା ଜଣାପଡୁଛି ଆମ ଡ୍ରାମା ପାଇଁ ସେ ପୁରା ଫିଟ୍।' 'ନାନୀ, ସେ ଆଗରୁ କେବେ ଡ୍ରାମା କରିଛି?' 'ସେଥିରୁ କଣ ମିଳିବ, ମୁଁ ତାକୁ ଶିଖାଇ ଦେବି। ଦେଖିବ, ସେ କେମିତି କମାଲ୍ acting କରିବ।' ନାନୀଙ୍କ ଭବିଷ୍ୟତ ବାଣୀ ସତ୍ୟ ହେଲା। ସମସ୍ତଙ୍କୁ ଅବାକ କରି ଝିଅଟି ତା'ର ନିଖୁଣ ଅଭିନୟରେ ଦର୍ଶକମାନଙ୍କୁ ଅଭିଭୂତ କରିଦେଲା। କେହି ବିଶ୍ୱାସ କଲେ ନାହିଁ କି ଏହା ତା'ର ପ୍ରଥମ ଅଭିନୟ ଥିଲା। ଖାଲି ଡ୍ରାମା ନୁହେଁ, କେଉଁ ପିଲା ଗୀତ ଗାଇ ପାରିବ, କେଉଁ ଗୀତ ତା' କଣ୍ଠରେ ଭଲ ଶୁଭିବ, ସେ ସବୁର ଅନୁମାନରେ ନାନୀଙ୍କର କେବେ ଭୁଲ ହେବାର ମୁଁ ଦେଖି ନାହିଁ।

ସେଇ ଅନନ୍ୟ ପ୍ରତିଭାଙ୍କୁ ମୋର ସହୃଦୟ ଶ୍ରଦ୍ଧାଞ୍ଜଳି:

ବନ ଲତା ସିଏ ବନରେ ନ ହଜି
ଜୀବନେ ସୁଷମା ଭରି
ନିଜ ଗୁଣେ ଗୁଣୀ ଗୁଣକୁ ଚିହ୍ନାଇ
ଅସମୟେ ଗଲେ ଝରି ।

■

ଆମ ଲତା ଅପାଙ୍କର କିଛି ଅଭୁଲା କୀର୍ତ୍ତି

ଆରତୀ ଓ ନୃସିଂହ ବିଶ୍ୱାଳ

ଯେମିତି ସତ୍ୟର ଶେଷ ନାହିଁ ସେପରି ଲତା ଅପାଙ୍କ ଚରିତ୍ରର ବର୍ଣ୍ଣନା କଲେ ତାହାର ଆରମ୍ଭ କେଉଁଠି ଅନ୍ତ କେଉଁଠି ଜଣାପଡେ ନାହିଁ। ଆଜି ଆମର ଅନୁଭୂତିକୁ କିଛି କଥା ଏବଂ କବିତାର ପଂକ୍ତି ରୂପେ ଉପସ୍ଥାପିତ କରିବା ପାଇଁ ଚେଷ୍ଟା କରିଛୁ। ତାଙ୍କର ବ୍ୟକ୍ତିତ୍ୱ କେବଳ ଚିତ୍ତ ଆକର୍ଷକ ନଥିଲା ମନୋରଂଜିତ ମଧ୍ୟ ଥିଲା।

ଲତା ଅପା ସଦା ବନ୍ଦନୀୟ, କେତେ ରୂପ ତୁମରି
ସେନେହ ମମତାର ସାଗର, ଅଟୁ ସର୍ବଶ୍ରେଷ୍ଠା ନାରୀ
ବିନା ସ୍ୱାର୍ଥେ ସମର୍ପିଲ ନିଜକୁ, ପ୍ରଜ୍ୱଳିତ କରି ଚଉପାସ
ଚାଲିଗଲ ଏକା ଟେକିଦେଇ ମଥା, ହୃଦେ ଦେଇ ପ୍ରୀତି ପରଶ
ଜନନୀ, ଭଗିନୀ ଜାୟା ତିନି ରୂପ ଏକ କାୟା:-

ପ୍ରସବ ବେଦନା ନେଇ ସନ୍ତାନ ଜନ୍ମ କରି ନଥିଲେ ସତ କିନ୍ତୁ ନିଜ ବାତ୍ସଲ୍ୟ ମମତା ନିସ୍ୱାର୍ଥ ପ୍ରେମ ସାହାଯ୍ୟ ଓ ସହଯୋଗ ମନବୃତି ଯୋଗୁଁ ଶହଶହ ଓଡ଼ିଆଙ୍କ ଜନନୀ, ଭଗିନୀ ଭାବେ ବନ୍ଦନୀୟ ଥିଲେ।

ନିଜର ଭାବି ତୁମେ ଧୈର୍ଯ୍ୟର ସହିତ ସହିଲ ଆମର ଅଳି
ଆଦରରେ ପରକୁ ଆପଣାର କଲ, ସେନେହର ଅମୃତ ଢାଳି
ଅନ୍ୟକୁ ସାହାଯ୍ୟ କରିବା ପାଇଁ ଦେଇଅଛ କେତେଯେ ସୁଖର ଜଳାଞ୍ଜଳି
ଧନ୍ୟ ତୁମ ନିଷ୍ଠା ହୃଦୟେ ପୂଜିତ ଘେନ ଆମର ଶ୍ରଦ୍ଧାଞ୍ଜଳି।

ସୌନ୍ଦର୍ଯ୍ୟର ପୂଜାରିଣୀ:-

ଆମ ଲତା ଅପା ଥିଲେ ସୌନ୍ଦର୍ଯ୍ୟର ପ୍ରତିମୂର୍ତ୍ତି। ଅପାଙ୍କୁ ପ୍ରଥମ ଦେଖାରେ ହିଁ ଭାଇନା ବାହା ହେବାର ନିଷ୍ପତ୍ତି ନେଇଥିଲେ। ନିଜ ସ୍ୱାସ୍ଥ୍ୟ ଖରାପ ଯୋଗୁଁ wheel chair ବ୍ୟବହାର କରୁଥିଲେ କିନ୍ତୁ ତାଙ୍କର ବୟସ କିମ୍ବା ଅସୁସ୍ଥତା ତାଙ୍କର ସୌନ୍ଦର୍ଯ୍ୟତାରେ କିଛି ପ୍ରଭାବ ପକାଇ ନଥିଲା, ସେ ସଦା ସବୁ ଝିଅଙ୍କୁ କହନ୍ତି, ତୁମେ ନିଜ ଚାକିରି, ଘର, ପିଲା ଏବଂ ପତିଙ୍କ ଛଡା ନିଜ ପାଇଁ ମଧ୍ୟ କିଛି ସମୟ ବାହାର କର, ନାରୀର ସୌନ୍ଦର୍ଯ୍ୟତା ନାରୀର ମନବଳ ଏବଂ ଦମ୍ଭକୁ ବଢ଼ାଇ ଥାଏ।

Ray-Ban ଚଷମା ପିନ୍ଧି, wheel chairରେ, ଆସନ୍ତି ଆମ ଲତା ଅପା
Estee Lauder କ୍ରିମ ଲଗାଇ , ଫିକାକରି ଦିୟନ୍ତି ଗୋଲାପର କୋମଳତା
Salon ଯାଇ shining, କରନ୍ତି ନିଜ ବାଳ, ନଖର ସୁନ୍ଦରତା
ସୌନ୍ଦର୍ଯ୍ୟର ପ୍ରତୀକ ସ୍ନେହ ଶ୍ରଦ୍ଧାର ପୁଜାରିଣୀ ହେଲେ ଆମ ଲତା ଅପା

କଳା ସଂସ୍କୃତିର ସଂରକ୍ଷିକା:

ଲତା ଅପା ଜଣେ ଓଡ଼ିଆ କଳା ପ୍ରେମୀ ଥିଲେ, ସେ ଏକ ନିଖୁଣ ଅଭିନେତ୍ରୀ, ନିର୍ଦ୍ଦେଶକ, ଏବଂ ଓଡ଼ିଆ ଶାସ୍ତ୍ରୀୟ କଳା ସଂସ୍କୃତିର ସଂରକ୍ଷଣ କରିବା ପାଇଁ ସଦା ତତ୍ପର ଏବଂ ନିରନ୍ତର ଉଦ୍ୟମ କରିଥିଲେ।

ଫକୀର ମୋହନଙ୍କ Patent Medicine ନାଟ୍ୟରେ ମୁଖ୍ୟ ଅଭିନେତ୍ରୀ ହୋଇ ନାରୀ ଅବଳା ନୁହଁ ଆବଶ୍ୟକ ହେଲେ ନାରାୟଣୀ ହୋଇ ନିଜ ପରିବାର ସଂରକ୍ଷଣ କରି ପାରିବ, ଶିକ୍ଷା ସମାଜକୁ ଦେଇଥିଲେ। ରେବତୀ ନାଟ୍ୟରେ ମୁଖ୍ୟ ନିର୍ଦ୍ଦେଶିକା ହୋଇ ପାରମ୍ପରିକ ପ୍ରଥା ଏବଂ ଲେଖକଙ୍କ ମନ୍ତବ୍ୟକୁ ଅତି ସୁନ୍ଦର ଭାବରେ ଲୋକଲୋଚନକୁ ଆଣିଥିଲେ। ଆଜି ମଧ୍ୟ ମନ ପଡୁଛି ତାଙ୍କର ଉପଲୋଚନା, 'ଆଲୋ ରେବତୀ ପୋଇ କୋଳି ଓଠରେ ନ ଲଗାଇ ତୁ କାହିଁକି lipstic ଲଗାଇ ଥିଲୁ।'

Face time ନାଟ୍ୟର ନିର୍ଦ୍ଦେଶିକା ହୋଇ ଅଭ୍ୟାଷ ସମୟରେ ଭାଇନାଙ୍କୁ ବାରମ୍ବାର କହୁଥିଲେ 'ହଇଓ ବୁଝିଲ, ତୁମ ଦ୍ୱାରା କିଛି ହେବନି, ଭଲରେ ଘୋଷ ନଚେତ ତୁମେ ମଂଚ ଉପରେ କେବଳ ଠିଆ ହେଇକି ଆସିବ'। ଅତି ସ୍ନେହ ଆଦରରେ କାହାକୁ ଖଣ୍ଡା ଖାଇ କହୁଥିଲେ ତ କାହାକୁ କଡା ଆଦେଶ ଦେଇ କହୁଥିଲେ 'ତୁମର ଏତେ ଦୁଃଖ ଅଭିନୟ, ତୁମେ କଅଣ ହସୁଛ।'

ଓଡ଼ିଶାର ଲିଭି ଯାଉଥିବା ଶାସ୍ତ୍ରୀୟ ସଂଗୀତ ଓଡ଼ିଶୀ ଚମ୍ପୁ ଛାନ୍ଦ ଯାହା ଧୀରେ ଧୀରେ ଲୋପପାଇ ଯାଉଥିଲା ତାହାକୁ ବଞ୍ଚାଇ ରଖିବା ପାଇଁ ନିରନ୍ତର ପ୍ରୟାସ କରିଥିଲେ। ବିଭିନ୍ନ ଚମ୍ପୁ ଛାନ୍ଦ CD ମାଧ୍ୟମରେ ପ୍ରବାସୀ ଓଡ଼ିଆଙ୍କୁ ସଂଗୀତ ସାଧନା ପାଇଁ ପ୍ରେରିତ କରିଥିଲେ, OSA Convention ଏବଂ NYNJPA କୁମାର ପୁର୍ଣ୍ଣିମାରେ, ଚମ୍ପୁ ଛାନ୍ଦ କାର୍ଯ୍ୟକ୍ରମ ମୁଖ୍ୟ ସଂଗୀତ ପ୍ରଦର୍ଶନ ଭାବେ ଆରମ୍ଭ କରିଥିଲେ

ଏବଂ ପ୍ରତ୍ୟେକ participantsଙ୍କୁ କୃତଜ୍ଞତାର ଭେଟ ସ୍ୱରୂପ ନିଜ ତରଫରୁ କିଛି ଅର୍ଥ ଦେଇ ପୁରସ୍କୃତ କରୁଥିଲେ। ଆଜି ମଧ୍ୟ ସରଦ୍ୱୀନ୍ଦୁ ଭାଇନା ସେହି ପ୍ରଥାକୁ ନିଭାଉଛନ୍ତି। ଅପାଙ୍କର କଳା ସଂସ୍କୃତିକୁ ବିକାଶିତ କରିବାର ଅଶେଷ ପ୍ରୟାସ ସବୁବେଳେ ସମସ୍ତ କଳାପ୍ରେମୀଙ୍କ ହୃଦୟରେ ଅମର ହୋଇ ରହିଅଛି।

ଜନମି ତା ବୁକୁରେ ବିକାଶିଲୁ ତା ସଂସ୍କୃତି ଦେଶ ଦେଶାନ୍ତରେ
ସତ ପ୍ରୟାସ କରି ଚମ୍ପୁ ଛାନ୍ଦ ଓଡ଼ିଶୀକୁ ସଂରକ୍ଷିଲୁ ପ୍ରବାସୀ ଭିତରେ
ପାଶ୍ଚାତ୍ୟ ଦେଶରେ ଶାସ୍ତ୍ରୀୟ ସଂଗୀତର ସ୍ୱର ଗୁଂଜୀଲା ଘରେ ଘରେ
ଗରବିଲା ଓଡ଼ିଆ ମାର ଛାତି ତୋ ନିସ୍ୱାର୍ଥ ସେବା କର୍ମରେ।

■

ପ୍ରଣାମ ଲତା ନାନୀ -ଏକ ଅନନ୍ୟ ଆତ୍ମା

ଶ୍ୱେତପଦ୍ମା ଦାଶ

ପ୍ରଣାମ କରୁଛି ଆମ ଲତା ନାନୀଙ୍କୁ,
ଏକ ନିର୍ଭୀକ, ଅନନ୍ୟା, ଅବିନଶ୍ୱର ଆତ୍ମାଙ୍କୁ,
ପ୍ରଣାମ କରୁଛି ଆମ ଲତା ନାନୀଙ୍କୁ।

ତାଙ୍କ ଉଲ୍ଲସିତ ହସ
ତାଙ୍କ ହୃଦୟର ଦୃଢ ବିଶ୍ୱାସ
ତାଙ୍କ ଓଡିଶୀ ସଙ୍ଗୀତର ସ୍ୱର
ତାଙ୍କ ସ୍ନେହଭରା ସ୍ମୃତିର ସମ୍ଭାର
ତାଙ୍କ ସୃଜନ ଶକ୍ତିର ସିନ୍ଧୁ
ତାଙ୍କ ସମର୍ପିତ ଆତ୍ମା ବିନ୍ଦୁ
ତାଙ୍କ ନାଟକ, ଆଉ ଅଭିନୟ
ତାଙ୍କ ସ୍ୱର, ତାଳ, ଆଉ ଲୟ
ତାଙ୍କ ଓଡ଼ିଶା ସଂଗୀତକୁ ବଞ୍ଚାଇବା ଶପଥ
ବିଦେଶୀ ଓଡ଼ିଆଙ୍କୁ ଦେଖାଇଥିଲା ପଥ।

ପ୍ରଣାମ କରୁଛି ସେ ଅନନ୍ୟ ଆତ୍ମାଙ୍କୁ,
ଆମ ଲତା ନାନୀଙ୍କୁ।

ସେ ଭଲପାଉଥିଲେ ଆମ ଓଡ଼ିଆ ସଂସ୍କୃତିକୁ
ଓଡ଼ିଆ ପରଂପରା, ଛାନ୍ଦ ଆଉ ଚମ୍ପୁକୁ
ବାଧା ବିଘ୍ନ ତାଙ୍କୁ କରିପାରିନଥିଲା ଶୀତଳ
ଜୀବନ ସଂଗେ ଲଢ଼ି, ଅନ୍ତରୁ ପାଇଥିଲେ ବଳ
ସ୍ୱପ୍ନ ତାଙ୍କର ହୋଇଥିଲା ସଫଳ
ଶୁଦ୍ଧ ସଂଗ୍ରାମର ପାଇଥିଲେ ଫଳ
କରାଇଲେ ପ୍ରତିଯୋଗିତା ଏ ଆମେରିକାରେ
ଓଡ଼ିଶୀ, ଛାନ୍ଦ, ଚମ୍ପୁ ଓଡ଼ିଆ ସଂଗୀତରେ
ବଞ୍ଚାଇ ରଖି ପାରିଲେ ଓଡ଼ିଶା ସଂସ୍କୃତି ଏ ବିଦେଶରେ
ଏଠାରେ ଜନ୍ମ ନେଇଥିବା ପିଲାଙ୍କ ମଧୁର କଣ୍ଠରେ।

ପ୍ରଣାମ କରୁଛି ସେ ଅନନ୍ୟ ଆତ୍ମାଙ୍କୁ,
ଆମ ଲତା ନାନୀଙ୍କୁ।

କେମିତି ବିଧାତା ଯୋଡିଥିଲା ସେ ଦୁହିଁଙ୍କୁ
ଲତା ନାନୀ ଓ ବିଶାଳ ହୃଦୟ ଶଶୀ ବାବୁଙ୍କୁ
ଜଣେ ଥିଲେ ଶବ୍ଦ ତ ଅନ୍ୟ ତାର ସ୍ୱର
ଜଣେ ଥିଲେ ବାଦ୍ୟ ତ ଅନ୍ୟ ତାର ଝଙ୍କାର
ଦୁଇ ଦେହ ଦୁଇ ମନ ହେଲେ ଏକା ପ୍ରାଣ
ଦୁଇ ଆତ୍ମା ର ଥିଲା ଅପୂର୍ବ ମିଳନ
ତାଙ୍କ ଦୁହିଁଙ୍କର ସ୍ନେହ ମମତା ବନ୍ଧନରେ
ବାନ୍ଧିହେଲେ ବିଦେଶୀ ଓଡ଼ିଆ ଏକ ପରିବାରରେ
ସେମାନେ ହେଲେ ସମସ୍ତଙ୍କର ଅତି ଆପଣାର
ସ୍ନେହ ବନ୍ଧନରେ ବଂଧା କେହି ନୁହେ ପର।

ପ୍ରଣାମ କରୁଛି ସେ ଅନନ୍ୟ ଆତ୍ମାଙ୍କୁ,
ଆମ ଲତା ନାନୀଙ୍କୁ।

ତାଙ୍କର ମଧୁର ଅମର ସ୍ମୃତି
ତାଙ୍କର ଅବିନଶ୍ୱର ଆତ୍ମା ଜ୍ୟୋତି
ଜଳୁଅଛି, ଜଳୁଥିବ ଦିନ ରାତି
ତାର ହେବନାହିଁ, କେବେ ଇତି ।

ପ୍ରଣାମ କରୁଛି ସେ ଅନନ୍ୟ ଆତ୍ମାଙ୍କୁ,
ଆମ ଲତା ନାନୀଙ୍କୁ ।

■

କାଲିଫର୍ଣ୍ଣିଆ

BLACK EAGLE BOOKS

www.blackeaglebooks.org
info@blackeaglebooks.org

Black Eagle Books, an independent publisher, was founded as a nonprofit organization in April, 2019. It is our mission to connect and engage the Indian diaspora and the world at large with the best of works of world literature published on a collaborative platform, with special emphasis on foregrounding Contemporary Classics and New Writing.

www.ingramcontent.com/pod-product-compliance
Lightning Source LLC
Jackson TN
JSHW081456270326
99965JS00011B/13

* 9 7 8 1 6 4 5 6 0 8 5 3 0 *